NOTTI ....

TALES OF MYSTERY
AND MURDER

Nottinghamshire Tales of Mystery and Murder

David Haslam

COUNTRYSIDE BOOKS
Newbury, Berkshire

First published 2002
© David Haslam 2002

COUNTRYSIDE BOOKS
3 Catherine Road
Newbury, Berkshire

To view our complete range of books,
please visit us at
www.countrysidebooks.co.uk

ISBN 1 85306 720 2

Produced through MRM Associates Ltd., Reading
Printed by J. W. Arrowsmith Ltd, Bristol

For Mincie and Harry

Contents

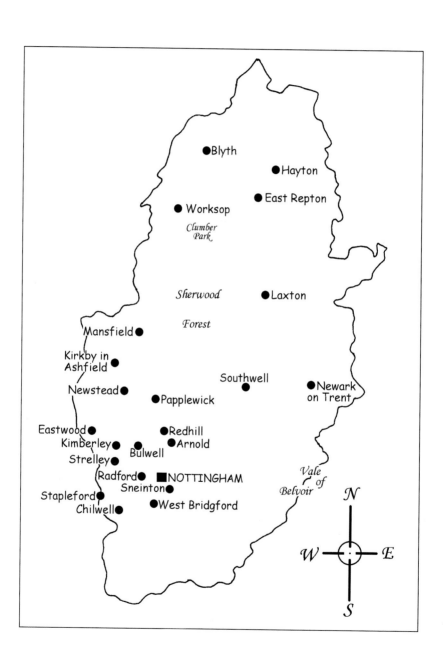

THE HAUNTED ORCHARDS OF NORWOOD PARK

The Owl shrieks around thee, as in wild despair,
All the restless spirits of the night
Own thee their deity, and love to share
Those thick wove horrors that shrink from the light.
With thee the dark and gloomy raven dwells,
Alone by day, and coins his mystic lore;
Or unseen elfins weave their guileless spells,
Which our rude fathers dreamt in days of yore.

(From a poem by 'Beta', entitled 'Lines on an Old Oak in
Norwood Park, Near Southwell', that appeared in *'The
Student.'* Or *'The Midland Counties Literary Repository'*
No. 5, 1838.)

Norwood Park, on the outskirts of Southwell, was
originally one of the medieval deer parks belonging to
the Archbishops of York. Mr John Sutton built the present
house in 1763. Today, this fine Georgian mansion is the
home of Sir John and Lady Starkey and the centre of a
commercial fruit farm. The house is periodically open to the
public, displaying 17th and 18th-century family portraits
and fine Victorian furnishings. Visitors seeking an encounter
with the supernatural in the house will be disappointed;
according to Sir John, the house has never been haunted.
However, walkers and cyclists on 'The Woodland and

Orchard Trail', which winds through the park, should pay particular attention to the orchards and fruit farm, since, according to some of the farm workers, they *are* haunted.

Pam, Pearl and Janet have worked on the fruit farm for many years. Pam and Pearl are sisters, with more than a drop of Romany blood in their veins. These are the very last people one expects to indulge in morbid speculation, yet their experiences on the estate, and those of others they have worked with, have led them to believe that there are ghosts in Norwood Park.

In the midst of the orchards, in the old walled garden, is the Pack House. Here the fruit is processed, packed and dispatched to customers throughout the country. Whilst working here late one night, Pam and Janet had a most eerie experience. 'We had to stop late one night packing strawberries. I had felt a presence that made me look up. I saw something gliding across the ground. It was like a long misty white, smoky shape. It had no feet. It went right across the yard towards the indoor office. I wasn't frightened as such but I wasn't very happy about it either. I'm normally

Norwood Park is the home of Sir John and Lady Starkey, and the centre of a commercial fruit farm. (Courtesy of Ron Wood)

very tanned but I went as white as a sheet. Janet must have seen the look on my face because she followed my gaze and she saw the tail end of this thing. The other girls kept asking what was the matter. I wouldn't tell them for fear the younger ones would all go home and leave me to finishing packing the strawberries! So, I told Carol, one of the women, and she said, "You've seen the ghost of Edward Cludd. We've heard him many times making noises at night, but we've never seen him." Much later, one night I went out of the Pack House for a smoke. I felt this presence again and heard a low murmuring sigh. I had this cold feeling around the back of my neck, just like a bee or a moth flying round you, but there was nothing there. My niece Dawn also felt this icy draught around her and heard the sighing. It really frightened her.'

Janet confirmed this: 'I saw this white shape go past the door of the Pack House, just as Pam described it. I also felt that presence before, a sad, solemn feeling.'

Had Pam and Janet seen the ghost of Edward Cludd? Cludd was a Justice of the Peace, and a Knight of the Shire for the county of Nottingham. He bought Norwood Park in 1646, where he built a 'lordly pleasure house'. This was demolished in 1763 to make way for the present building. As part of his civic duties he conducted marriages, said to have been held in Norwood Park under a mightly oak that became known as 'Cludd's Oak'. The oak has long since gone; the remains were still to be seen in 1881, lying in 'gnarled and aged pieces amid the flowers of May and the luxuriant undergrowth of a picturesque plantation.' Though a staunch supporter of Cromwell, Cludd prevented local people from carting away the stone from the Minster during the Civil War. He was too late to save the canon stalls and the Archbishop's throne, and the Archbishop's Palace was pulled down for timber and stone. Cludd's actions probably saved the fabric of the Minster. If the townsfolk had got to the lead on the roof the Minster could well have been made a ruin.

The Pack House is not the only scene of weird happenings in Norwood Park. Pearl explained, 'In Haylam orchard there is a mischievous spirit. It appears like a bright light that dashes in and out of the trees just like a child playing. It looks like a torch but moves too quickly. It follows you about as you work and moves from tree to tree. We've all seen it. In Lodge orchard, in the middle section towards the bottom, is a horrible presence. As if someone were watching you, following you. You can get this feeling all day working in there.'

In 1990 Pam, Pearl and Janet were winter pruning in Haylam orchard. Pam described what happened: 'We're on piece work rates when we do the winter pruning and I had told Janet to go back along the row and count the number of trees she'd done. I bent down to finish off a tree. I could see someone standing behind it in the next row. I could see this black shape and the feet beneath the tree. I thought it was Janet and told her again to go back and count the pruned trees. When I straightened up there was Janet some way off, coming towards me. I couldn't believe it. "How have you got there?" I said, "I've just been talking to you." She explained she'd been back to count the trees as I asked. So I don't know what it was.'

North Park orchard was also said by the staff to have an ominous atmosphere; even the men don't like it there. Although this orchard has been dug up, there remains an eerie atmosphere. Staff have noticed a lack of wildlife; no rabbits or pheasants amble through the tress there and no birds sing. In winter 1984 Pam and Pearl, along with other staff, Ann, Margaret and Rita, were busy with winter pruning. There was no wind blowing but suddenly some dry leaves were swept up in a spiralling mass. The workers were quite spellbound by the sight. Then Margaret, a most down to earth person not known to take flights of fancy, spoke, 'Hello m'duck. Where has he gone?' 'Who?' her friends asked.

'The man standing there,' she said. 'He was wearing a brown coat, sandals and had his hands folded in front of him.' The others had only seen the swirling leaves. Margaret was obviously shaken. She was off work for three months after this incident. In the same orchard two ladies fell from ladders within days of each other when their ladders were inexplicably moved. This also happened to Pam, who was left hanging from a branch when her ladder collapsed under her, as if pushed over.

Why the orchards of Norwood Park are haunted is a mystery. The fruit farm began as 10 acres in 1910 and has grown from there. Could it be that the spirits amidst the trees are shades from Norwood's more distant past and not connected with the orchards themselves? Fruit, especially the apple, has an important role in folklore beliefs. In many apple-growing regions the orchards are still wassailed in the autumn. Local people gather together, with perhaps Morris dancers and music, and go into the orchards. Libations of drink, usually cider, are consumed and poured onto certain trees. Shotguns are fired up into the branches, often accompanied by loud renditions of traditional wassailing songs. The aim of wassailing the fruit trees seems clear – to ensure that the trees thrive and to frighten off evil spirits. The farm workers at Norwood Park would most likely welcome an excuse to raise a glass in the orchards; and should Sir John make wassailing a regular event he might well be rewarded by higher yields.

THE HOLLINWELL
INCIDENT

On Sunday 13th July 1980, at the Hollinwell Show, hundreds of people were suddenly stricken by a mystery illness. A fleet of ambulances ferried 259 of the worst affected casualties to four area hospitals. At the time, everything from nerve gas to high frequency radio waves was suspected. The official report on the incident found that mass hysteria was the likely cause, a conclusion that MP Dennis Skinner called, '. . . an insult to the intelligence and another cover-up by the Establishment'. Many people agreed with him. If this wasn't mass hysteria, then hundreds of children and adults were felled by an agent undetected by medical science that has still not been identified.

The show was held in a field near Kirkby in Ashfield, just off the A38 near Hollinwell Farm. It featured a competition of junior brass and marching bands. Many of those attending had travelled far by coach to arrive in time for the 9.30 am start. Around 11 am the bands were called to order to await inspection by the judges in the arena. Just before midday the band members standing in rank began to collapse, first in ones and twos then by the dozen.

A police officer attending said, 'The kids went down like ninepins.' What had been a happy scene at a summer show was transformed. An eye witness later told reporters, 'Some kids were catching their friends as they fell, and then they were falling themselves. No one could understand what was happening. . . It was like a battlefield with bodies everywhere.' Terry Bingham, one of the show organisers, described the scene: 'We were ready for display when one or two children collapsed. Then a few more went, and a few more. We called off the event but others fell as they came out of the arena. Then spectators started dropping.' Amongst the symptoms reported were fainting, running eyes, sore throats, dizziness, vomiting, trembling, weakness, numbness and a metallic taste in the mouth.

One of the girls affected was Paula Merriman, who was 14 at the time. She told reporters, 'We were on the field in full uniform for an inspection . . . I've never had to stand to attention for that long before. As we marched off I tried to grab hold of my drum but just fell on the floor. My friends were collapsing all around me.' Another casualty was Kerry Elliot, who was 10, 'I just went all weak and got pains in my stomach and then I fainted. Everyone was falling down and some were crying. My stomach was all tight and aching. I felt better when I came round in hospital. . .' Her seven year old brother Steven was also affected. Linda Elliot, the mother of Kerry and Steve, was taken ill as she went to hospital with her children. 'My arms and legs felt like sponges and it was like cramp in my stomach. That's all I remember until I came round.' Mrs Edna Wells, chairperson of one of the bands, The Ashfield Imperials, tried to keep the ill children talking, '. . . I was helping them and then I was taken ill too.' According to the *Daily Star* of 14th July two horses were also affected – a significant detail in the search for the cause of the mystery illness.

Of the 259 people taken to hospital fifteen were adults. Nine casualties were detained in hospital overnight – seven children and two babies. Some adults were taken ill as they accompanied children to hospital and others fell ill in the wards and at the bedsides of those admitted. Terry Bingham said his own eyes began to sting and water as he drove six children to hospital in his car. 'I had chest pains. It was like nerve gas poisoning.' Margaret Palethorpe, the mother of three children who collapsed, said she suffered pins and needles in the tongue and lips. Her symptoms got worse: 'I collapsed and lost the use of one arm.'

Police and public health officials were quickly on the scene. In order for the medical authorities to treat the growing number of casualties the cause of the illness had to be found quickly. There was no way of knowing at this stage how serious the outcome of this illness might be. Food poisoning was the immediate suspect. An announcement over the public address system warned people not to eat the ice cream or drink the water until the cause of the illness was found. This was followed by a warning about bottled mineral waters to the same effect.

Police and health officials took samples from all the food and drink from all the vendors at the show. The Severn Trent Water Authority tested the water supply. However, it quickly became apparent that this was a blind alley; many of those affected had brought their own food and drinks with them. The test results proved negative anyway. By the end of the day officials were able to report that no bacterial impurity had been found in any likely source.

A second theory emerged: mass poisoning by some noxious substance. The immediate suggestion was that chemical insecticide sprayed on the field had poisoned the crowd. There was speculation that the feet of the crowd had raised into the air dust containing some chemical irritant. However, police on the scene tracked down the owner of the field, who told them that it hadn't been sprayed for fourteen years.

Adding to speculation, spokesperson at the Queen's Medical Centre at Nottingham said that children treated there seemed to show symptoms that '. . . were consistent with exposure to fumes of some kind.' It was suggested that poisonous fumes could have come from a fire at a plastics factory, which had happened some six miles away. However, urgent inquiries found that the wind had been in the wrong direction to have spread toxic fumes to the show and that the fire was too distant to have caused the symptoms seen at the show. Further to this, a light plane had been seen in the area in the previous days. It was suggested that the plane had been spraying the nearby Nottingham Golf Course. Immediate investigation at the club found this not to be the case. This didn't stop the *Daily Mirror* reporting on its front page the next day: 'Gas Cloud KOs Kids'.

News of the incident spread rapidly through the national media. A man in Scotland contacted local police suggesting that high frequency radio waves could be the cause. There was just such a transmitter at a nearby gas depot, but this line of inquiry was eliminated.

By the end of that dramatic day police and health officials had drawn a blank. At an evening press-briefing Inspector Eric Hogden said: 'The whole thing is a complete mystery. Food poisoning and mass hysteria have definitely been ruled out.'

Away from the deserted showground, more incidents were occurring. During the night of 13th/14th July five of the children released from hospital were re-admitted when their symptoms reccurred. On 16th July a married couple and an eight-year-old girl collapsed with similar symptoms and were taken to hospital. According to the *Daily Mail* of the 17th none of them had been affected on 13th July. On 19th July six children from Ashfield Imperials, one of the bands involved in the Hollinwell incident, fainted during a charity walk at South Normanton. On the 20th July five girls from the Kilton Concords, another one of the bands at the Hollinwell incident, fell ill during a charity event.

From the moment the Hollinwell incident hit the national media speculation was rife. Even as the ambulances ferried the casualties away and well before official agencies had reached any informed opinion, experts began to give their conclusions to the waiting press, despite the lack of evidence and with little reference to the ongoing situation on the ground.

Apart from one suggestion that the Coxsackie virus, known to be epidemic in the area and whose symptoms are a mild illness with chicken pox like blisters, was responsible for the illness (this theory was discounted as the virus was thought unlikely to cause such a dramatic reaction), the opinions on the cause fell into two camps: mass hysteria and chemical poisoning.

Although local police and health officials had made no mention of mass hysteria being the cause, several newspapers began to liken the Hollinwell incident to many other, similar, events that had taken place in schools and colleges, factories, offices and nurses' homes whose cause had been attributed to mass hysteria. In common with the Hollinwell incident they had been blamed initially on food poisoning, fumes or toxic chemicals; but then, when no evidence of these was found, mass hysteria was said to be the cause and the events quickly and conveniently forgotten.

On 16th July the *Daily Telegraph* concluded, 'Tests indicate that the cause was nothing more than mass hysteria . . .' This conclusion suggests that because tests had found no obvious cause, mass hysteria must be the explanation. It was only after this newspaper article was published that Dr John Wood, Director of Health for the Kirkby area, said he was becoming convinced that mass hysteria was the only possible conclusion as all the tests had eliminated all the alternatives. He told reporters, 'Part of it may have been one or two getting ill and the rest getting hysterical. A large number of small children had been parading and standing to attention for some time. They would also be under pressure due to the occasion.'

Writing in the *Guardian* in January 1980 before the Hollinwell incident, Brian Inglis had focused on popular misconceptions with regard to mass hysteria: 'Hysteria can imitate the symptoms of a range of physical, physiological and neurological diseases. This includes symptoms of toxic poisoning.'

The mass hysteria explanation angered those affected, parents and organisers. Terry Bingham called it, 'Rubbish. There has been a cover-up. Some people are still feeling ill . . . So how can it have been hysteria?'

Supporters of the mass hysteria theory suggested that the long wait the bands had in hot and humid conditions had brought on the symptoms. However, according to one witness, Mrs Maureen Reville, 'There was no hysteria. People didn't collapse all together. It was cool enough a day for most of us to have our coats on. . .' (*Daily Star* 17th July). The detail that two babies and several horses fell ill also seemed to counter the mass hysteria explanation. The stricken horses were mentioned in the first radio bulletins of the incident. The *Sunday Times* said that following the show five horses were taken ill and one had to be destroyed. This was later denied by the show organisers and didn't feature in police reports.

Regarding the evidence for poisoning, it was reported in The *Guardian* on 15th July that traces of blood and protein had been found in some of the children's urine samples, possibly indicating kidney damage. However, which hospital this information came from is not mentioned. At a news conference Dr Malcolm Lewis, head of Nottingham Public Health Laboratory, said that tests on blood and urine samples for organo-phosphorus poisoning had all proved negative.

The *Daily Mirror* offered contradictory facts on 23rd July. It was reported that Kirkby in Ashfield health officers had found traces of '. . .a cocktail of cleansing fluid and diesel fumes' at the site, which they believed contributed to the mystery illness. This seems an oddly inaccurate description from trained scientists; a cocktail of fluids and fumes makes no sense. Where was this cocktail found – in the air, in dust from the ground? How did the casualties come into contact with it? This in turn was contradicted by reports in news-papers on 24th July, which stated that tests by Kirkby in Ashfield authorities had found no traces of toxic agents whatsoever.

An article in the *New Statesman* agreed that, deliberately or not, local authorities had indeed been involved in a cover up. This had been an incident of poisoning by organo-phosphorus compounds as present in pesticides commonly used in agriculture. The article highlighted the fact that around 50 brands of such pesticides were derived from nerve gas formulas. Terry Bingham claims that on his release from hospital he steamed open the letter from the hospital to his GP. Mr Bingham found the diagnosis was 'inhalation of organic poison'. It was further claimed that mass hysteria could not account for the lingering and recurring symptoms and that pesticide poisoning could. In response to these allegations of a cover up, the Ashfield District Council published their report. However, their inconclusive findings didn't satisfy local opinion.

In a follow up letter to the *New Statesman* on 31st July Dr R H Lawson voiced his own misgivings about the mass hysteria explanation. He wanted to know the results of any tests for cholinesterase levels in the blood and protein in urine. He mentioned the possibility of a number of girls menstruating at the time of the incident being a factor in the search for an answer. Crucially, Dr Lawson suggests that the hysteria versus poisoning argument is not mutually exclusive, '. . . since one of the symptoms of organo-phosphorus poisoning is anxiety, and it is theoretically possible that the threshold for hysterical conversion in the crowd may have been lowered by a physical agent.' In other words, people were poisoned.

When trying to solve a mystery it is wise to choose the simplest solution however improbable that solution may seem to be. Is mass hysteria the explanation here or is this an attempt to 'explain away' events? Could hysteria generated at the Hollinwell Show have lingered for days, affecting both adults and children after the event? And what of the reccurrence of symptoms? The mass hysteria explanation appears reassuringly straightforward; comforting, almost. The alternatives are disturbing. Were hundreds felled by an agent undetected by medical science? Was there a cover up? Following the revelations about Gulf War Syndrome and other public health scandals, official explanations are not accepted on face value as they once were. The official report is available on request at local libraries. Local people may have stopped asking questions but they haven't forgotten the Hollinwell Incident.

THE MURDER OF
BESSIE SHEPPARD

Where the A60 runs through Thieves Wood some two miles south of Mansfield is a weather-beaten stone at the road side. The inscription on the stone has all but gone over the years but a glance at a map will tell you that this is 'Sheppard's Stone', the scene of a gruesome murder.

Bessie Sheppard left home at Papplewick on the morning of 7th July 1817 to walk to Mansfield. She was looking for work as a domestic servant. She wore her new shoes for the occasion and carried a brightly coloured cotton umbrella. She got the job and was seen leaving Mansfield at around 6 pm on her return journey home. She never arrived.

All that same day Charles Rotherham of Sheffield had been drinking heavily. The one-time scissors grinder's apprentice and ex-soldier was seen at the Hut Tavern, Newstead, near the crime scene on the evening the murder took place. It seems that Bessie simply happened to be in the wrong place at the wrong time. Rotherham beat her to death after she passed him on the road, using a hedge stake that he found nearby. In a frenzy he searched the body for money, but found none and so stole the only items of value on her person, her shoes and her umbrella.

The next morning, 8th July, some quarry men on their way to work found Bessie's mangled body in a ditch by the roadside. According to a contemporary broadsheet, she had been so savagely attacked that her features were unrecognis-

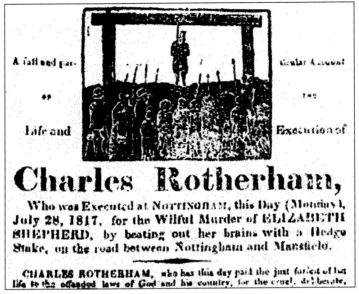

A full and par-   cicular Account

Life and   Execution of

Charles Rotherham,

Who was Executed at NOTTINGHAM, this Day (Monday), July 28, 1817, for the Wilful Murder of ELIZABETH SHEPHERD, by beating out her brains with a Hedge Stake, on the road between Nottingham and Mansfield.

CHARLES ROTHERHAM, who has this day paid the just forfeit of his life to the offended laws of God and his country, for the cruel, deliberate,

According to the broadsheet, Bessie had been so savagely attacked that her features were unrecognisable.

able, the brain protuded from the skull, and one eye was completely knocked out of the socket and lay on the cheek. Shocked and horrified the workmen stopped a couple riding by in a gig. From their higher vantage point in the gig, the couple could clearly see the ghastly scene and the blood-stained hedge-stake near the body. They set off in haste to inform the police at Mansfield.

After committing the murder, Rotherham had tried to sell Bessie's shoes at a hostelry called the Ginger Beer House. There were no takers. He proceeded to the Three Crowns Inn, Redhill. Here, according to the old broadsheet, he sang two songs and again attempted to sell the pitiful booty. There were no buyers and he left the shoes in his room at the inn. The umbrella was eventually sold in the village of Bunny on the other side of Nottingham. Rotherham walked to Loughborough. He was standing on a canal bridge looking into the water when a constable approached him and arrested him. Rotherham made no attempt to escape and went along quietly.

After his arrest Rotherham made a full confession. He could give no reason for the murder but want of money for drink. He said he hit Bessie with the hedge stake and kept hitting her until she was dead. A large crowd gathered at Gallows Hill in Nottingham to see Rotherham hanged for his crime and cheered as he kicked out the last of his sorry life at the end of the rope.

As an expression of the public sympathy Mr Anthony Bukles and some other Mansfield worthies commissioned a permanent memorial to the sad fate of Bessie Sheppard. At the spot where the body was found a stone was set up with the following inscription: 'This stone was erected in the memory of Elizabeth Sheppard, of Papplewick, who was murdered by Charles Rotherham, near this place, on the 7th of July 1817, aged 17 years.' When the A60 was widened the stone was moved and re-erected on the new verge. Local folklore has it that Bessie's ghost has been disturbed as a result. Since that time local newspapers have periodically reported sightings of Bessie's ghost on the A60.

THE MYSTERIOUS
NED LUDD

'No more chant your old rhymes about bold Robin Hood
His feats I do little admire.
I'll sing the achievements of General Ludd,
Now the hero of Nottinghamshire. . .'

These words from the old folk song 'General Ludd's Triumph' celebrate the Luddite rebellion of 1811. We now use the term 'Luddite' to mean someone who hates progress. The original Luddites were opposed to new production methods which put them out of work and condemned their families to misery and hunger. But who was their mysterious leader?

In 1811 Nottinghamshire hosiery manufacturers began to receive letters signed by a General or King Ludd. Little was known about Ludd, though his name carried the weight of armies. Workers who had seen their wages reduced and their jobs taken by unskilled labour began breaking into factories and destroying machines. Their main targets were the new wide frame knitting machines operated by unapprenticed labourers.

In Arnold, near Nottingham, Luddites stole the jack wires out of the knitting frames during the months of February and March. The jack wires were desposited in unnamed local churches as 'hostages', but the owners did not cave in to the demands of the 'hostage' takers. On 11th March an angry crowd of framework knitters gathered in the market place at Nottingham. The crowd was so large that local officials called in the militia to disperse them. That evening some 60 knitting frames belonging to blacklisted manufacturers were broken in Arnold. In the weeks that followed more knitting frames were broken and the attacks became more widespread. By April over 200 frames had been destroyed and 400 special constables sworn in to protect the factories.

A lull in the attacks lasted until the night of November 4th, when six wide frame machines were destroyed in the village of Bulwell. On November 10th a mob led by someone calling himself Ned Ludd broke into the knitting shop of Edward Hollingsworth – 'a notorious and hated hosier' and destroyed several of his machines. On 13th November a great mob of workers from Hucknall, Kirby, and Bulwell wrecked many of the knitting frames at Bett's Workshop. Luddite bands would gather, in the darkness of the night, in the forests surrounding the towns and villages. The attacks were well organised: armed men, often masked, would storm a target factory. Outside the owner would be restrained and his workers discouraged from interfering by a show of force. The machines were then smashed with hammers. Once their mission was accomplished the Luddites would disappear before the authorities could give chase. By the end of November 1811 they were so emboldened as to launch daylight raids.

That same month the magistrates of Nottingham told the public 'There is an outrageous spirit of tumult and riot. Houses are broken into by armed men, many stocking frames are destroyed, the lives of opposers are threatened, arms are seized, haystacks are fired and private property destroyed.' The Prince Regent offered a £50 reward for information about those, '. . .wickedly breaking the frames'.

Those in authority believed Ludd to be a real person. They refused to acknowledge that mere stockingers could

WHEREAS,

Several EVIL-MINDED PERSONS have assembled together in a riotous Manner, and DESTROYED a NUMBER of

FRAMES,

In different Parts of the Country :

THIS IS

TO GIVE NOTICE,

That any Person who will give Information of any Person or Persons
thus wickedly

BREAKING THE FRAMES,

Shall, upon CONVICTION, receive

50 GUINEAS

REWARD.

And any Person who was actively engaged in RIOTING, who will
impeach his Accomplices, shall, upon CONVICTION, receive the
same Reward, and every Effort made to procure his Pardon.

☞ Information to be given to Messrs. COLDHAM and ENFIELD.

Nottingham, March 26, 1811.

*The Prince Regent offered a £50 reward for information about those
'. . . wickedly breaking the frames'.*

organise themselves and carry out such effective acts of protest. The Luddite activists were happy to maintain this illusion, disguised their true identities, and, like Robin Hood and his Merry Men, met in secret in Sherwood Forest. 'King Ludd' wrote to the Prime Minister Spencer Perceval, '. . . in consequence of the great suffering of the poor – whose grievances seem not to be taken into the least consideration by government – I shall be under the necessity of again calling into action my brave Sons of Shirewood. Who are determined and serious to be true and faithful avengers of their country's wrongs.' Such sentiments would not have been out of place in a medieval ballad spoken by Robin Hood himself. In a letter to the Home Office the Luddites claimed ancient rights to protect their livelihoods in the form of a charter from Charles II. In such correspondence the Luddites often gave their address as 'Sherwood Forest'.

In February, 1812, as Luddism spread north, Spencer Perceval's Government passed the Frame Breaking Act, which carried the death sentence; 12,000 troops were ordered into the affected areas. Adding to the tumult, the poet Byron used his maiden speech to the House of Lords to defend the Luddites and speak against the Frame Breaking Bill. Byron's political views were expressed in his poems, *Songs for the Luddites* (1816) and *The Landlords' Interest* (1823).

Parliament sent a squadron of Dragoons to Nottinghamshire to assist the local militias but this did not deter the Luddites. By 15th December 1811, the county was host to an army of some 900 cavalry and 1,000 infantry, led by General Dyott. By early 1812 Parliament feared a French-style revolution taking hold and sent Lieutenant General Thomas Maitland and a force of 35,000 men to crush the Luddites in the north. During that violent summer of 1812, Luddites were executed and more transported to Australia. By December 1812 the attacks had ceased. There were a few more sporadic attacks up to 1816, but, to all intents and purposes, General Ludd had retired.

Where did the Nottinghamshire stockingers get the idea for General, or King, Ludd from? Some say he was Ned Ludd, an apprentice of Anstey in Leicestershire, who had taken a terrible beating from his master. In revenge Ned Ludd smashed his master's knitting machine with a hammer. Despite the best efforts of researchers no proof for this story can be found. The Luddite rebellion began in Nottinghamshire not Leicestershire, so the story of Ned Ludd seems apocryphal. So where did the name come from?

The earliest source on King Ludd is the work of Henry of Huntingdon, which Geoffrey of Monmoth drew on for his *History of the Kings of Britain*, written in the twelfth century. Monmouth's Ludd was an ancient British King of Trojan descent who succeeded his father, Beli or Belinus. King Ludd is said to have built a defensive earthwork from Daventry to the North Sea, north of the Wash. He also built a 'New Troy', later called Luddein or London, in his honour. Ludd is said to be buried beneath Ludgate in London. Ludd's Gate, a great arched gateway, survived until the Great Fire, in 1666. In the Midlands, Lud's Church is a rocky chasm in the Black Forest above the Dane valley in Staffordshire. This is where Sir Gawain is said to have faced the Green Knight. There is also a famous white stone, Luddenden Dean, in West Yorkshire, said to be freshly painted by persons unknown every May Day morning as part of a continuing secret Celtic tradition.

The roots of this story go much deeper. King Ludd is a humanised form of a much older deity. According to *The Encyclopaedia of Myths and Legends of all Nations*, by Robinson and Wilson, Ludd is the son of Don, the British Celtic god of the sun. In *Everyman's Dictionary of Non-Classical Mythology* Ludd is the British name for Nudd, or Nuda, the King of the Tuatha de Danaan, the Faerie people. In the Welsh myths of *The Mabinogion*, Ludd or Nudd, son of Beli, father of Gwyn and lord of Annwfn, has a fairy palace at Glastonbury.

Could Nottinghamshire hosiery workers have known any of this? It seems too far removed from their reality. Or were the stockingers far more in touch with story telling, songs and myths than we imagine? Or was it simply blind chance that Nottinghamshire stockingers took the name of an ancient god for their leader?

It becomes even more curious when one reads the myth about King Ludd ridding the land of three plagues. The first of these was the invasion by the Coranieid, a tribe with magical powers. The Coranieid could hear every word that was borne on the wind; their currency was fairy money that appeared good at first but turned into dry leaves. The second plague took the form of a hideous shriek, heard throughout the land, striking everyone with fear and foreboding. The third plague caused food from the royal stores to disappear without trace. This seems like an allegory of what industrialisation was doing to the stockingers: taking away their source of income and security and depriving them of cheap food.

The power of mythology to energise and rally people has been seen many times in history and the Luddites were very aware of this power; one Luddite writer describes Sheffield as a City of Vulcan. King Ludd is an example of people in rebellion using a collective identity. The Luddites were inspired by and consciously borrowed from the myths of Robin Hood. It is curious that Nottinghamshire should create two archetypal figures both fighting for the poor against social injustice. You only have to describe someone as a Luddite or acting as a 'Robin Hood' and people will understand precisely what you mean. Sherwood Forest must be fertile ground for growing heroes. The truth about Ned Ludd – vengeful apprentice boy or ancient Celtic god – remains veiled in good Sherwood mist.

The Demons Within

In the early hours of the morning of 17th January 1998, 53-year-old Brian Wade walked down the hill from his flat in Burns Street, Radford to Central Police Station. Reporting to the desk, he dropped a bloodied machete, an eight-inch knife and a Dictaphone onto the counter. Wade was covered in blood; the route he had taken from his flat to the police station was marked by splashes of blood. Wade had come to turn himself in after killing a man. A trivial incident had unleashed the personal demons that he had controlled for years. This was a preventable tragedy; if the authorities had listened to Wade's complaints about noise from the flat below, and if this seriously mentally ill man had been given better supervision and support, then perhaps Jonathan Abell might not have been killed that night. Brian Wade was a walking time bomb and no one heard him ticking.

A psychologist giving evidence at the trial said Brian Wade suffered from an untreatable psychotic personality disorder. This condition causes paranoia and extreme sensitivity to criticism. The illness often made Wade feel as if people were 'out to get him' and he could errupt into violent anger at times of stress.

Brian Wade had a troubled upbringing and blamed his problems on an 'unhappy' early life. He told Nottingham Crown Court that his mother had endured 30 years of domestic violence before 'dying a broken woman' in a mental hospital. In his youth Wade's mental condition and the violence it

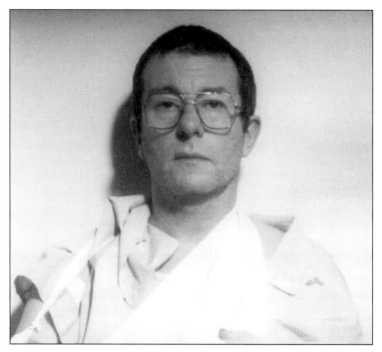

Brian Wade turned himself in to the Central Police Station in Redford, dropping a machete, a knife and a Dictaphone on the reception desk.

engendered brought him before magistrates some 92 times. In 1966 Brian Wade murdered a neighbour in circumstances similar to those of the murder of Jonathan Abell that he committed 32 years later.

In 1966, 21-year-old Brian Wade lived next door to Edwin and Betty Cardwell and their two children in Wood View Place, Canklow, Rotherham. Edwin Cardwell, 45, worked shifts as a burner in a steelworks and had had his sleep disturbed by Wade's revving of his motorbike outside his home. He had spoken to Wade about this, and on the evening of 15th July Wade had been brooding on these complaints whilst drinking heavily.

At around 1 am on 16th July Wade forced the back door of the Cardwell's home and crept upstairs. Psychosis and drink had unleashed demons in Brian Wade. He dragged Edwin Cardwell from his bed and smashed in his skull with a sledgehammer. Betty Cardwell was woken by a loud thump, which she took to be her husband falling out of bed. Reaching for the bedside light, she saw her husband, covered in blood, dying from terrible head injuries. The sledgehammer lay by the bed. Brian Wade had fled the scene. Minutes after the attack Wade told a policeman that he might have killed a man. Tried at the Sheffield assizes, Wade was sentenced to life imprisonment.

Prison life did nothing to help Wade's mental state. In 1971, five years into his sentence, Wade was stunned to read in the *News of the World* that his brother and sister-in-law, aged 21 and 19, had committed suicide, leaving an 18-month-old baby. The following year, he stabbed a fellow inmate in Wakefield Prison nine times with a pair of scissors and was sentenced to ten years for wounding.

In 1984, Wade was freed from prison on a life sentence parole and moved to Burns Street, Nottingham. He formed a relationship with Tracy Gray, and they had a son. Acquaintances said he was pleasant, though intense and quiet. Police officers and probation officers described Wade as intelligent and polite. A local resident said of Wade: 'If you met him in the street you would not think he was capable of [*murder*]. He is a very intelligent man. One time he broke into a bike lock in a few seconds. He took it down to Raleigh to show them.'

He made no secret of his previous convictions. Being out on life sentence parole meant that he found work hard to come by, but he did odd jobs for pensioners in the Arboretum and Radford areas.

Wade still struggled with his personal demons. He created a refuge – which he described as an 'an oasis of peace and comfort' – in his Burns Street flat. A prey to his mounting paranoia, Wade had a six-inch-deep steel door on the flat. He also kept a machete. Wade feared that his life licence, handed to him when he was released from goal, would be revoked if he got into trouble.

In July 1997 Tracy Gray, with the couple's son, moved out of Wade's flat in Burns Street. That same month Helen Williams and boyfriend Geoff Smith moved into the flat below; they created problems with noise almost immediately. Wade complained to the police and local authorities that he was plagued by loud music, shouting and banging from the flat below. He started keeping a log and recording the nuisance on a Dictaphone. Experts later found that the volume of music was twice the recommended acceptable level. As well as complaining a number of times about the music Wade also alleged that Miss Williams' dog had fouled the stairs of the flat. Describing Wade before he killed Abell, a neighbour told the court 'Brian seemed nervous when we saw him. Some problems with people in the flat were getting to him quite badly.'

Occasionally Mr Abell stayed overnight with Helen Williams and her boyfriend and visited several times between December and the day of his death. Jonathan Abell was described as a 'lovable rogue'. The 22-year-old from the Bestwood Estate, Nottingham, had been in trouble for burglary and car crime and had served a short prison sentence for assault committed in Skegness, where he worked as a holiday camp security guard. Jonathan was well known and well liked in Radford and the Arboretum area.

On the day of the murder Wade was woken around 4.40 am by loud music. Jonathan Abell was visiting his friends in the flat below, he had been drinking and put on a Phil Collins record. Wade took himself for a walk, returning to his flat about 5 am, picking up his Dictaphone and an eight-inch bread knife. He switched on the Dictaphone to record the noise and went downstairs. Wade then removed the fuse from the electrical box, plunging the flat below into darkness and silencing the music. Jonathan Abell, who didn't like the dark and was claustrophobic, went upstairs demanding Wade replace the fuse. Wade was waiting at the top of the stairs. A violent argument broke out and Wade repeatedly stabbed Abell with the bread knife. Leaving Abell bleeding on the stairs Wade returned to his flat to fetch a machete, with which he hacked him a further 16 times. Forensic evidence showed that Wade had wounded Jonathan Abell 49 times with the machete and bread knife.

From her flat Helen Williams heard Jonathan Abell beg for help. At the trial she told the court 'I saw Brian Wade hanging over him and just slicing him with a knife. It must have been a long knife because it looked like he was cutting a piece of meat. He had no remorse. It was horrible.' The Dictaphone in Wade's pocket recorded the screams of 22-year-old Jonathan Abell as he was hacked to death. At the trial the screams of the dying man were played to the hushed court.

His defence lawyers suggested that Wade had lashed out with the knife fearing that Abell was carrying a weapon. In cross examination Helen Williams was asked whether Jonathan Abell had threatened to kill Wade when they passed in the street after he complained about the noise. Miss Williams said: 'No'. Wade's defence sought to establish whether Jonathan Abell ever carried a weapon. The court was told that Mr Abell carried a screwdriver several times. Asked by prosecution whether Jonathan Abell had carried one when confronting Wade on the night of the murder, Helen Williams answered, 'No'.

As he had done 32 years earlier, immediately after killing Edwin Cardwell, Wade turned himself in. However, this wasn't the end of the investigation, conducted by a team of twelve detectives led by Detective Chief Inspector Chris Barnfather, of the major crime unit. After the trial DCI Barnfather told reporters, 'This was not a case where we were without a suspect. Wade walked down the hill from his flat to Central Police Station after killing his victim and dropped the weapons and the Dictaphone on the counter.

But that is not where the investigation ends. We had to make sure every piece of evidence we collected stood up in court for a prosecution. We could not cut any corners and have weaknesses in the case.' The first step was to secure the scene. There were splashes of blood all along the road from the flat to the police station indicating the way Wade walked. We had officers guarding these as well. We had to swab nails, knives, walls, everything. Although Wade admitted the killing straightaway, we have to work on the assumption that there might be some other explanation put forward for us to prove or disprove. Wade might have denied it a month later. We keep working, tightening the case, even when the court hearing is ongoing. I would say that this is one of the most gruesome cases I have worked on.'

Sentencing Wade, Mr Justice Poole said it was a 'brutal killing' and despite the history of loud music from the flat below, 'Nothing justifies the measures you took when you savagely attacked him, first with a knife then with a machete.'

In court Wade said, 'This young man should never have died. I am not immune to this kind of thing. I have a little boy. Somehow this young man got through the barriers and I just cracked and broke. I'm sorry, I'm sorry, I'm sorry.'

Wade was again jailed for life at Nottingham Crown Court with a recommendation he serve at least 15 years. Wade could be freed in 2013 if the parole board decides to allow him out on licence. By then he will be 68 years old.

The widow of Wade's first victim, Edwin Caldwell, told

Reporting to the desk, Wade dropped a blooded machete and a six inch knife onto the counter.

reporters: 'We feel so incensed. He is so obviously a danger to the public. We were not aware he had been released. We thought he was in Broadmoor as he is a maniac.'

Mr Abell's father, Patrick, said after the trial, 'He should never have been let out. Wade was a walking time bomb. You have got to give people a chance to make good but the second time, when he stabbed the inmate, they should have realised he was so dangerous. I fear he will be released from prison in a few years and somebody else could be killed.'

Care in the Community was introduced by the Conservative Government in 1981 and resulted in a number of high profile killings by mental patients. In the five years before the Wade case there were five instances in Nottinghamshire of mental patients killing someone after being released. The saddest case was probably that of schizophrenic Anthony Smith, who stabbed his mother Gwendolyn and 11-year-old half-brother David at their home in Sandiacre. Anthony Smith had been released from Derbyshire Royal Infirmary for just a month. The Department of Health is still trying to find a way of getting violent people with psychological disorders off the streets. The government promised new legislation to tackle this issue, but as the law stands at present those with an untreatable personality disorder cannot be sectioned under the Mental Health Act.

MYSTERY IN THE DUNGEONS

On a cold September morning I stood looking up at the southwest tower of Newark castle. I had been asked by an archaeologist friend, Nicola Jennings, to look at some strange carvings in two bottle-shaped dungeons dating from between 1290 and 1320. There was a suggestion that some of the carvings looked Masonic and as a member of a local lodge I was asked to take a look.

The warden of the castle led us through narrow, dimly lit corridors of ancient stone work. At the end of a gently downward sloping passageway we encountered two shafts, sheer drops of some 5 metres into the bowels of the castle, entry points for two dungeons made with no way out. If the fall didn't kill the poor soul dropped down from above then neglect often did. Dungeons like these are called *oubliettes* from the French 'to forget'; prisoners were simply thrown in and forgotten about. Here on the stone work above the entrance to the first chamber were some of the mysterious carvings. We were intrigued by what we saw. At about knee height is a carving of a ladder measuring about 25 cm high and 5 cm across. A hand-held light showed the words 'W in the Kist'. Cryptic to say the least. A kist is a stone box or structure made to safeguard something valuable, like a relic. Nearby is a ship with a high prow beneath open compasses, below this the name 'Robert' in stylised carved script. There are wheels, spiral forms and, strange grid-like patterns,

Newark castle (Jenny Challis)

which reminded me of 'Nine Men's Morris'. The castle warden also showed us another dungeon on the far side of the castle with Templar crosses, more wheels and an impressive bird of prey or raven clutching what could be a globe or disk in its talons. But now it was time to go down into the dark.

We descended into the first dungeon by means of a modern wooden ladder fixed to the wall. This chamber is approximately 9 metres high and 4 metres in diameter at its widest point. The walls are lined with a brick skin that stands proud of the original wall by about 3 inches. The brick skin had been breached in one place about 1 metre up from the floor. This breach is quite precise, as if whoever made it knew what lay beyond. Above the hole one can just see a ladder and some indistinct initials scratched onto the brick. Beyond the breach is a curious niche cut into the original wall. The back wall of the niche had been painstakingly carved out to form a cross in relief. Flakes of red paint still adhere to the stonework of the cross. Our first thoughts were of the red cross of the Knights Templar. If I had been standing in a church rather than a dungeon I would have called this credence, where the host is placed ready for the Eucharist. Closer examination showed that the niche had a shelf or mantle beneath, pierced with holes about as wide as a man's thumb and about as deep as to the first knuckle; candle holders perhaps?

I was full of questions; had someone made a hole in the brick to retrieve something from the niche behind the wall? How did they know the niche was hidden here? Did the ladder carving in the corridor show the way to the ladder scratched on the brickwork in the dungeon?

If the first chamber is intriguing the second is awe-inspiring. The second chamber is about 8 metres high, 3 metres 20 cm across and bottle shaped. No brick skin covers the original stone walls here. All sound is muffled. A glimmer of natural light leaches in from a single high window so narrow the air can barely squeeze through.

This chamber has five niches. Each has a cross carving at some state of completion. Some of the niches have holes in the mantle shelf. All the niches show some evidence of smoke blackening within them, some more than others. The niches are fanned out on approximately two thirds of the circle of the wall, as if facing west. The niches are on average 120 cm apart, centre to centre. No two niches have exactly the same dimensions: two are 38 cm and 33 cm high and 31 cm wide, respectively; the other three are slightly smaller, between 26 cm and 30 cm high and between 25 cm and 28 cm wide. On the wall facing the niches, at just above head height, is a larger aperture attributed to the work of squatters in the 18th century.

This looks and feels like a place of worship or ritual rather than a dungeon. Though not decorated or constructed for display the honest construction of the chamber shows great care and the stonework of the domed ceiling is impressive. The entry point is through the 'shoulder of the bottle'. The chamber is dry and cool, the earth floor dusty. There is a ridge or stone corbel running round the wall some 40 cm above floor height, as if to support a wooden floor above the existing earth floor. One of our party used this edge as a foothold to gain height, his voice boomed around the chamber, although he hadn't raised his voice – a demonstration of the strange quality of the acoustics in the chamber.

We took photographs, compared notes and began our ascent. We wondered, is the first chamber like the second, with many more niches around its wall behind the brick skin? We could still only conjecture about these intriguing chambers. Could they be the work of the Knights Templar? Who were the Knights Templar and what connection did they have with Newark?

The Knights Templar were an order of warrior monks formed to protect Christian pilgrims en route to the Holy

Ladder carving above a chamber (Jenny Challis)

Land. The order became wealthy and powerful, building castles across Europe and the Middle East, operating its own fleet and acting as moneylenders to kings. Some historians attribute the invention of the banking system to the Templars.

Legends and mystery surround the Knights Templar. Whole libraries are filled with books on their exploits in battle, their downfall, their hidden treasure, and on their alleged mastery of occult knowledge. Some claim the Templars have influenced everything from freemasonry to the drafting of the American constitution. However, behind all the smoke and mirrors we can rely on surviving documentary evidence to tell us about the Templars in Newark and the surrounding area.

The historian Cornelius Brown tells us in his *History of Newark* that the Templars had property in the town before 1185. The order is said to have had a hospital on Stodman Street, Newark with its own chapel. The Lincoln inquisition of 1311 tells us '. . . the Masters and Brethren of the Knights Templars had in Newerk 2s. of annual rent . . . from William Drye 12d. and from Matilda formerly wife of Mathew de Bankwell 12d.' The Templars owned lands at Collingham, Sibthorpe, Syreston, Spaldeford and Gretton. The 1311 inquisition also tells us, '. . . at Thorpe by Newark three oxgangs of land . . . worth 44s. per year. They had in the township of Stoke 2s. 3d. Rent, viz. From Geoffrey Osbern.' The Templars also had an important preceptory at nearby Eagle.

The Templars' wealth was the cause of their downfall. By 1307 King Philip the Fair of France was desperate for money for the war against England. On Friday 13th October, 1307 King Philip had all the French Templars arrested on grounds of heresy. This was the only charge that would allow Philip to seize their money and assets. Subsequently, under torture, French Templars confessed to blasphemy, trampling and spitting on the cross, homosexuality and sodomy, wor-shipping a demonic idol called 'Baphomet', worshipping a calf, worshipping a cat and practising sorcery. The Templars were a truly international organisation and Philip needed the support of other crowned heads and the Pope. It was only after Pope Clement V issued bulls abolishing the order that Edward II of England reluctantly moved against the Templars, in 1310 issuing the order to arrest the English Templars and seize their property. In 1311 trials were held at York, Lincoln, and London.

Records tell us the knights were held in the gatehouse of Clasket Gate in Lincoln. The Bishop of Lincoln, John de Dalderby, was one of the commissioners appointed for the trial. Newark was one of the Bishop's castles and it is possible that Templars were held there. The surviving Lincoln Inquisition records of 1311 give us a glimpse of our local Templars. Among those examined was Brother Richard de Colyngham, who said he had not worshipped any calf, but had promised to be obedient and live chastely and without personal property and protect the Holy Land. Brothers Thomas de Burton and Thomas de Staunton, 'being repeatedly exhorted that they should leave the order, answered what they would rather die.' So too said Thomas de Ludham, William de Thorpe, William de Pocklington, Robert de Colyngham and John de Stoke. The Bishop of Lincoln ridiculed the charges and declined to take further proceedings against the Templars.

However, more confessions on the continent brought more trials. Under pressure from the papacy the English church fell into line. The Provincial Synod of Canterbury forced the knights into 'perpetual seclusion' within other monastic orders. The council of Vienne 1311 finally dissolved the order of the Knights Templar. On 19th March 1314 the last Grand Master, Jacques de Molay, was burned at the stake. No English Templars were executed.

Some time after visiting the dungeons I casually mentioned them to a work colleague, Miss Jenny Challis. I was frankly gobsmacked when she told me she had seen similar examples and began to reel off a wealth of specialist knowledge. Miss Challis, who had just completed a special study of Templar round churches for her BA dissertation, made a comparison between the dungeons and graffiti at Newark and other Templar sites such as the Royston cave, St Michael's church at Garway, and the dungeons in the Chateaux de Chinon in the Loire Valley, France. Miss Challis also pondered on whether the round dungeons at Newark could be connected in some way to the round Templar churches built in the same period.

Another visit to the Newark chambers, this time with Jenny Challis, was needed. Since my last visit the castle warden, Mr Rene Mouraille, had been doing his own research and a local archaeological group (The Farndon Archaeological Institution) had surveyed the chambers. Mr Mouraille believes that the chambers were always dungeons, not specially constructed ritual chambers. However, Mr Mouraille did surmise that they could have been used as comfortable accommodation for high-ranking prisoners, in what was then the newest part of the castle. Further to this, whoever made the graffiti and the niches had access to tools and may have been allowed to make the niches for some devotional purpose and to occupy themselves piously whilst captive. These prisoners must have found special favour with the bishop; they were, after all, digging into the walls of his newest dungeons. Could it be that some niches are more complete than others because the work on them was interrupted as the prisoners were taken off to trial? Mr Mouraille reserves judgement as the whether these prisoners were Templars held for the inquisition at Lincoln. The records for the Lincoln Inquisition of 1311 make no mention of Templar prisoners being held at Newark, but the records are incomplete.

After our second survey I visited Lincoln castle to check whether it had any features like those at Newark. Cob Hall at Lincoln castle was used as a dungeon, is of the right date and does indeed have some enigmatic graffiti protected under sheets of glass. At Newark some of the graffiti showed up best in a photograph taken with a camera flash. I photographed the stone work around the Lincoln graffiti. On viewing these photographs later I realised I had found another ladder motif with a horse next to it. The horse carving seems unfinished. This was an exciting moment – the same ladder graffito appearing in at least four places with Templar connections. But what did the ladder mean? There is a tradition that the nine humble knights who founded the Templars found some great secret beneath the ruins of King Solomon's Temple. Does the ladder refer literally to that perilous descent and discovery?

Sylvia Beamon, a research and writer on the Royston cave, draws some conclusions that may throw light on the Newark dungeons. She points out that Royston, like Newark, was a market town. The Templars would have needed to buy and sell at the market and Sylvia Beamon believes that the Templars used the Royston cave as a cool place to store their produce. We know one of the Newark chambers was used as an ice-house in the 18th century so it could have been used for storage long before that by local Templars. The preceptory at Eagle is seven miles by road from Newark and only three miles from the Trent, so goods could have come by boat straight to the castle. Sylvia Beamon argues that the knights would have also needed a chapel for their devotions. Could the dungeons at Newark have been used in a similar way, serving as sometime gaol, store house and chapel? Further to this, could the Bishop of Lincoln have allowed former Templars to use the dungeons for devotional purposes after the order was officially dissolved? Whatever use the castle dungeons were put to and what the enigmatic carvings really mean will remain a mystery until new evidence is uenarthed.

The White Lady of Newstead Abbey

The ghost of the White Lady haunts the grounds of Newstead Abbey, the ancestral home of Byron, our greatest romantic poet. Those who have seen the ghost in recent times describe her as dressed in white, with a little black bodice and a white hat with a veil that hides her face. She has been seen many times by the staff and visitors at the abbey and The White Lady Restaurant is named after her. But who was she?

The solution to this mystery begins with the poet himself. Byron's mercurial poetry made him the 'darling of London society'. He self dramatized himself as a man of mystery, as the archetypal brooding romantic figure; he made and broke the mould of the 'Byronic hero'. Byron's effect on women was as legendary as it was disastrous; he was 'mad, bad and dangerous to know'. Scandals, sexual and incestual, forced Byron to quit England in 1816. Debt, both inherited and accumulated, forced Byron to sell Newstead Abbey to Colonel Thomas Wildman in 1817. Roaming the Continent, settling only for two brief years in Venice, Byron produced some of the greatest poetry written in English, rejoicing in the human experience, celebrating its absurdity, cruelty, and its glory. In 1823 he joined Greek freedom fighters who had risen against the Turks. Lord Byron was struck by convulsions caused by marsh fever on 15th February 1824. He seemed to recover but an over zealous bleeding by doctors hastened a relapse. Byron died on 19th April at Missolonghi.

The impact of Byron's death on his public, especially his female public, was immense. When the sad news reached Mary Shelley, the young widow of fellow poet Shelley, she wrote in her diary of Byron, or 'Albe' as she knew him, *'Can I forget his attentions & consolations to me during my deepest misery? – Never. Beauty sat on his countenance and power beamed from his eye – his faults being for the most part weaknesses induced one readily to pardon them. Albe – the dear capricious fascinating Albe has left this desart world.'*

Mary viewed the body in London on July 9th. On 11th July Byron's old companion Hobhouse paid his last respects to his dead friend. On 12th July the huge London crowds saw the funeral cortège begin its four day journey to Nottinghamshire. Mary Shelley watched the procession as it passed her house. Lady Caroline Lamb broke down when she saw it. She was still infatuated with Lord Byron and remained notorious for her nine-months devotion to him in 1812. After the funeral procession she is said to have irreparably lost her mind.

John Clare, 'the peasant poet', wrote: *'While I was in London, the melancholy death of Lord Byron was announced in the public papers, and I saw his remains borne away out of the city on its last journey to that place where fame never comes. . . I happened to see it by chance as I was wandering up Oxford Street. . . when the train of the funeral suddenly appeared, upon which a young girl that stood beside me gave a deep sigh and uttered 'Poor Lord Byron.' . . . I looked up at the young girl's face. It was dark and beautiful, and I could almost feel in love with her for the sigh she had uttered for the poet. . . The common people felt his merits and his powers, and the common people of a country are the best feelings of a prophecy of futurity.'*

Clare later immortalised the scenes in his poem 'Byron's

Byron's effect on women was legendary: he was mad, bad and dangerous to know.

Funeral'. On 16th July 1824 Byron's coffin was finally laid to rest in the family vault at Hucknall Torkard. Byron's lasting fame was assured. His life, poetry and tragic early death had spawned a legend.

Later that same year, at the poet's ancestral home, the sister of Colonel Wildman was walking on the garden terrace at Newstead. She was suddenly surprised on the path by the spectral form of a woman in white advancing towards her. Apparently taking the figure to be a ghost, Miss Wildman, panic-stricken, turned and fled into the Abbey. Her encounter with the 'White Lady' caused lingering excitement on the estate.

Some days later Colonel Wildman received a letter; it was from the 'White Lady' herself. This was obviously no ghost! She had seen the Colonel's sister take fright at her approach and was sorry that she had inadvertently startled her. The 'White Lady' explained that she only wanted to wander the grounds because of her enthusiasm for Lord Byron. The Colonel paid the mysterious 'White Lady' a visit at her lodgings on Weir Farm.

She received him with some embarrassment, but he soon put her at her ease. Illness had left the 'White Lady' not only deaf and dumb, but with weak eyes and a frail constitution. She communicated by writing on a slate that she always carried with her. So it was that the Colonel came to know the story of this sad lady. She told him, via the slate, 'I am always amongst strangers, as much so in my native country as I could be in the remotest parts of the world. By all I am considered as a stranger and an alien, no-one will acknowledge any connection with me: I seem not to belong, nor to be regarded as belonging, to any human species.'

The 'White Lady' had been at Newstead some years, arriving shortly after Byron's sale of the estate to Colonel Wildman in 1817. While she never met the poet, her fascination with his life and works was totally absorbing. She was the daughter of a provincial book dealer, but now quite alone in the world, her parents dead and her only surviving relative, a brother, who was a captain of a merchant ship, in America. She lived off a small income provided from her father's estate, her brother being the executor. At that first meeting the Colonel learnt that the White Lady's name was Sophia Hyatt. Sophia always dressed in white, with a little black bodice and a white hat with a veil that hid her face. She would wander the estate for hours, standing for long periods under the tree where Byron had carved his name.

The Colonel, moved by the poor lady's situation, assured her the Abbey grounds were always open to her. On learning that the lady was virtually destitute, Colonel and Mrs Wildman took her welfare to heart and the Colonel sought, through his own business agents in Liverpool, to make inquiries into her brother's affairs in order to secure her rightful income. Mrs Wildman invited Sophia to the Abbey and let her use the library there.

The months passed with no response from America. Sophia's health and mental state declined. In a letter to the Colonel she wrote, 'I have long too sensibly felt the decay of my mental faculties, which I consider as the certain indication of the dreaded calamity which I anticipate with such terror. A strange idea has long haunted my mind, that Swift's dreadful fate will be mine – it is not ordinary insanity I so much apprehend, but something more terrible, absolute idiotism.' Sophia decided to leave Newstead for London so that she could start legal action in pursuit of her claim for her income.

On the day before leaving, Sophia gave Mrs Wildman a sealed packet with the instruction not to open it until she was gone. That evening Mrs Wildman opened the package to find letters and notes and all of Sophia's poems about Byron and Newstead. In the letter to Mrs Wildman herself Sophia fully explains her destitute position and the dreadful isolation her deafness had caused her. 'It is perhaps owing, in part at least, to the solitude in which I have lived, I may say even in the midst of society, when I have mixed in it, as my infirmities entirely exclude me from that sweet intercourse of kindred spirits . . . but since the loss of my hearing, I have always been incapable of verbal conversation . . .

You must have observed that I generally endeavour to

avoid both you and Colonel W. It was to spare generous hearts the pain of witnessing distress you could not alleviate ... I could not deny myself the indulgence, as you so freely gave me your permission, to continue my walks, but no. They are at an end. I have taken my last farewell of every dear and interesting spot, which I now never hope to see again, unless my disembodied spirit may be permitted to revisit them.'

Greatly moved by what she'd read Mrs Wildman's first impulse was to find a way for Sophia to stay on at Newstead. When Colonel Wildman immediately suggested that she could be given accommodation in one of the estate's new farm houses, Mrs Wildman wrote to Sophia that very night:

'Newstead Abbey, Tuesday night, Sept. 20. 1825.
Dear Madam,
Retiring to my bedchamber this evening, I have opened your letter, and cannot lose a moment in expressing to you the strong interest which it has excited both in Colonel Wildman and myself, from the details of your peculiar situation, the delicate and, let me say elegant language in which they are conveyed. I am anxious that my note should reach you previous to your intended departure from the neighbourhood, should be truly happy if, by any arrangement for your accommodation, I could prevent the necessity of your undertaking the journey, Colonel Wildman begs me to assure you that he will use his best exertions in the investigation of those matters which you have confided to him; and should you remain here at present, or return again after a short abscence, I trust we shall find means to become better acquainted, and to convince you of the interest I feel, and the the real satisfaction it would afford me to contribute in any way to your comfort and happiness. I will only now add my thanks for the little packet which I received with your letter, and I must confess that the latter has so entirely engrossed

An artist's impression of the White Lady, whose mournful spirit is said to wander the grounds of Newstead Abbey still.

my attention, that I have not as yet had time for the attentive perusal of its companion. Believe me, dear Madam, With sincere good wishes, Yours Truly, Louise Wildman.'

First thing the next morning a servant was sent to Weir Farm to deliver the letter. However, he returned to the Abbey with the news that the 'White Lady' had left for Nottingham, from where she would catch the coach for London. He was immediately dispatched to Nottingham to intercept Sophia. On reaching the town the road ahead was blocked by a crowd. Making his way through he came upon the body of the 'White Lady'. She had been struck by a coach and killed outright. Apparently, owing to her deafness, she had heard neither the approaching coach nor the warnings called out by several people. She was buried, at Colonel Wildman's expense, in the churchyard of Hucknall

Torkard, the resting-place of her beloved Byron. But, although laid to rest so near to her idol, it seems that poor Sophia did not find peace. Initially mistaken for a ghost by Miss Wildman, Sophia Hyatt did in fact come to fulfil that state of being. Her mournful spirit is said to wander the grounds of Newstead Abbey still.

THREE TIMES A KILLER

The circumstances surrounding the murder of Dawn Bersten belong in the squalid back streets of Victorian Nottingham not in the modern city of the 21st century; the characters involved in this case could have stepped straight from the pages of a Victorian 'Penny Dreadful'. It seems that advances in material wealth, mass education, communication and technology are simply not touching some people in our society, who live in a kind of twilight world.

John Cutts, a 45-year alcoholic, of St Ann's, Nottingham had a 20-year history of violence and criminality that has left three people dead. Forty-eight-year-old Mrs Dawn Bersten was an ill, vulnerable woman who neglected herself. She was described as a long-time friend of Cutts, indeed she was called his only friend. However, following an argument over a missing benefit book Cutts battered Dawn Bersten about the head with a bottle. He made no attempts to get Dawn, a diabetic, any medical aid; instead he took her to a friend's home and watched over her lingering death, some four days after the attack. When in January 2001 he was finally gaoled for the murder, the trial judge, Mr Justice Crane, told Cutts, 'You have an appalling record for violence.'

John Cutts has a string of convictions that plot his downward spiral, which ended in a life sentence. On 15th July 1982 Cutts was convicted for the manslaughter and

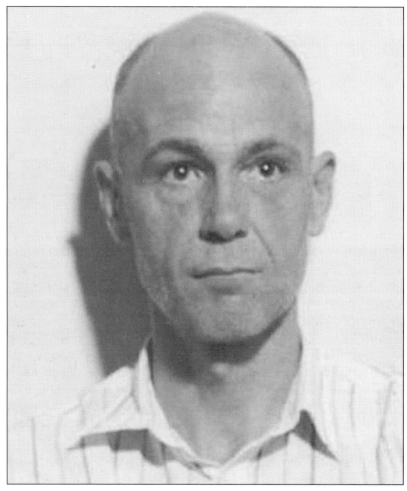

John Cutts, an alcoholic with a 20 year history of criminality which has left three people dead.

robbery of Mrs Lucy Flynn. Cutts, then 26, was one of a gang of three masked raiders who terrorised market traders Horace and Lucy Flynn at their home in Protester Road, Carlton. The gang rang the doorbell and forced their way in when 59-year-old Mrs Flynn answered. Mrs Flynn was kicked and punched to the floor. Alerted by her cries for help Horace Flynn ran downstairs armed with a wooden mallet. The masked gang then set upon him and knocked him unconscious with his own mallet. Mrs Flynn later died of a heart attack, brought on by the shock and trauma of the raid. Although Cutts was jailed for ten years he didn't serve the full term. His early release had tragic consequences. Not long after he was freed he caused death again. On 4th December, 1991, Cutts was convicted of causing death by reckless driving. He was gaoled for three and half years and disqualified from driving for ten years.

By 1995 Cutts was making life a misery for his neighbours in Heaton Close, St Ann's. In a statement to lawyers a resident said of Cutts: 'He made everyone's life an absolute hell. We tried to get him evicted because he was like a lunatic, causing so much trouble'. In 1997 Cutts was sentenced to 18 months for threatening to kill a former friend, Raymond Wilson, but was soon back in Heaton Close. Throughout 1998 his neighbours suffered constant problems of noise and abuse from Cutts and again complained to the council. When Cutts found out about the complaints he head-butted two people and smashed several windows, causing £200-worth of damage. Cutts admitted the offences and was given two years' probation on condition that he attend an anti-violence programme. This had no effect; Cutts was out of control. A catalogue of racist abuse and threatening behaviour towards neighbours followed and after making his neighbours' lives hell for over four years Cutts was imprisoned for a year in July 1999. His council flat was repossessed and he was banned from Heaton Close for two years. As soon as Cutts was released from prison he started loitering around Heaton Close once more.

Dawn Bersten lived in Ritson Close, St Ann's, near Heaton Close. Her health was collapsing. Although she suffered from diabetes she failed to medicate herself properly, nor did she seem willing or able to seek medical help. At the time of her death Dawn Bersten weighed just four and a half stones. On the night of the fatal attack, Cutts visited her with another man – James Murphy – who wanted to see Dawn because she owed him money. In court both men blamed each for what had happened next. At his trial Cutts told the court they had been at Mrs Bersten's flat for about an hour when Mr Murphy hit her. 'He was asking for dope and saying if she hadn't any dope then he wanted the money she owed him. He tried to pick her purse up and she told him to leave. I saw him hit her with a bottle.' Cutts said he then grabbed the bottle from Murphy and put it down.

In his evidence Cutts agreed that it had been his idea to take Mrs Bersten to Mr Murphy's flat because he said her home was 'a tip'. In evidence Cutts said, 'She put her coat on. We all walked back. Dawn fell over twice on the way. I supported her half of the way.' Once at Murphy's home in Heaton Close, Cutts bathed her and put her to bed. During that time both men say they checked on her and, over the following nights, Cutts had slept by her. Four days later, on 4th August 2000, Murphy found Dawn Bersten dead. A post-mortem examination revealed she had died of a combination of head injuries and a diabetic condition that can develop when sufferers go without insulin for a considerable length of time. 'A physical state like hers had hardly been seen since the introduction of insulin in 1922', said a medical examiner.

At the trial the prosecution alleged that it was Cutts who attacked Mrs Bersten. Murphy was initially charged with assisting an offender – a charge that was dropped at the beginning of the trial. The prosecution case hinged on proving that Mrs Bersten's death was ultimately caused by the injuries she suffered in the attack. Evidence emerged that Cutts had beaten Dawn Bersten in the past. A neighbour from Heaton Close gave testimony at the trial, describing Cutts' appalling treatment of his 'only friend': 'He reserved the worst treatment of all for Dawn, who seemed to be his only friend. He beat her black and blue. We used to worry that he was going to wind up killing her, the way he knocked her about. It's sad our fears came true.'

The jury heard during the case that Cutts' fingerprints were found on the murder weapon and Mrs Bersten's blood was found on his clothing. They returned a verdict of guilty to the charge of murder. Sentencing Cutts, Mr Justice Crane told him, 'This woman, who you described as a friend of yours, was attacked over a trivial matter. You took a bottle to the head of that unfortunate, wretched and very vulnerable woman.' With Cutts' record we can only hope that the life sentence he received protects the public from this man for a very long time.

THE BIG BLACK CAT

'The philosopher Ludwig Wittengenstein once said, the riddle does not exist. If a question can be put at all, then it can also be answered.'

When I was researching *Ghosts and Legends of Nottinghamshire* I came across reports of a black panther on the loose. Descriptions of the Nottinghamshire panther matched those of big black cats seen in places as far afield as Dartmoor, Wales and Scotland. My focus for that book was on folklore and the supernatural so I shelved the reports but added to them as I could.

Throughout Britain there are many old folk tales of terrifying black beasts wandering the countryside, with almost every county having at least one example. They are described variously as huge hounds, demonic wolves and occasionally as monstrous cats. The most famous of these is Black Shuck, the Suffolk Hell Hound. Conan Doyle's inspiration for *The Hound of the Baskervilles* was the folk tale of a phantom black dog on Dartmoor. In *Ghosts and Legends of Nottinghamshire* I wrote about 'The Boggan', the fearful Ghost Hound of Laxton. I found another example recently in a reference to a manuscript dated 1952 in the County Records. Here 75-year-old Mrs Smalley recalled that her grandfather (1804 to 1888) often saw a mysterious black dog on Crow Lane, between South Muskham and Bathley Round. It would appear from nowhere and trot alongside his pony and trap. Around 1915, Mrs Smalley's son Sidney also saw the black dog in Crow Lane when out on his motorcycle. He sometimes tried to run over it but was never able. One night both Sidney and his father saw the hound when they had gone out on the motorcycle with the express purpose of searching for it.

Phantoms or not, recent eye witness accounts seem to suggest that real, big, black felines are living in the wild and thriving. Big cat sightings have been made in the Bathley, Caunton and Norwell areas in recent years, according to Emerson of the Big Cat Society. On 24th April 1994 a black puma-like creature was seen chasing deer at Clumber Park near Worksop. Earlier that same day a similar animal was seen at Todwick, near junction 31 of the M1. Further north, at Finningley near Doncaster, it was seen again on 10th May and another sighting was reported in Sherwood Forest on 17th July. During that summer local newspapers reported sightings of a black panther in Sherwood Forest at Clipstone Pines.

At the time local forestry officials explained away the Sherwood sightings as being muntjac deer. The muntjac is about the size of a dog, and has unusual, canine-like teeth. A solitary, highly elusive creature, the muntjac has a curious motion when running, with its head down, rather like a big cat. Could the muntjac be mistaken for a big cat? Perhaps not, but it could alert observers to the presence of one. One forester at Clipstone Pines told reporters, 'If there was a large cat around then you would expect the local deer population to show signs. They would show signs of being disturbed and preoccupied.'

Three years later, in the summer of 1997, the big cat was on the prowl again. Following numerous reports from residents, armed police had been called to the village of Anston when a man walking his dog spotted a large feline predator in a tree. Muntjac deer don't climb trees. At the time of the incident a police spokesman said they had examined four-inch diameter paw prints left in mud. Anston residents told the local press that the animal was bigger than an Alsatian dog and pitch black in colour. According to the *Worksop Guardian* the big cat was picked up on security cameras in the Harworth colliery pit yard. Two more reports were also made in the Retford area at this time.

Then, on 20th June 1997 the *Worksop Guardian* featured the headline, 'Clumber Cat Paw Prints Are Analysed By Animal Experts.' The article features photographs of large paw printes found by market gardener Simon Ward in the grounds of Worksop College on the fringes of Clumber Park. Plaster casts of the tracks were made for forensic examination. Scene of Crime officer Graham Spencer told reporters, 'It might be a big dog and we are not animal experts so we might have to send them to the zoo department of Nottingham University. It's hard to say at this stage what they might be. They could be anything. The casts have claws and five pads.' The findings of this investigation went unreported and the trail went cold.

The following year animals matching the description of a black panther were seen in Derbyshire, Leicestershire, Lincolnshire and Nottinghamshire. In the summer it was seen in Stapleford Woods near Newark and at South Rauceby near Sleaford. In Sherwood Forest two large paw prints (5x4 inches), thought to be of the 'Beast of Bassetlaw', were found in August. Again, photographs and plaster casts were taken. This time the opinion of an expert did go on record: the paw prints were identified as puma or lynx prints by RSPCA inspector Steve Foster.

At 8.45 am on Saturday 1st May 1999 Mr and Mrs Legge saw the animal in a paddock at the back of their home in the village of Besthorpe, Nottinghamshire. Mrs Legge saw the cat from an upstairs window and called to her husband to come and see. Mr Reg Legge told *The Newark Advertiser* (7/5/99, page 2): 'It was about 40 yards from the house just sitting there on its haunches. It was sitting motionless

At 8.45 am, on Saturday 1st May 1999, Mr and Mrs Legge saw a big cat in a paddock at the back of their home in Besthorpe.

looking into the distance. It had quite a small head and a long black bushy tail. We watched it for about 30 seconds then it moved off. It was crystal clear, I just couldn't believe it.'

Mr Legge believes that his four dogs have been aware of the cat's presence for some time. 'Our dogs are pretty quiet, completely docile, and we let them out in the evening. But a lot of times lately they have gone absolutely mad, barking their heads off in a wild manner which is totally unlike them. When you add it up it begins to make some sense. Many people round here have got sheep and lambs and that's a concern. The cat is probably living off rabbits at the moment but it may go for the sheep.'

Mr Kevin Cunningham, the RSPCA's chief inspector for Nottinghamshire and Derbyshire, said the sighting of a big black cat by Mr and Mrs Legge was very credible. Mr Cunningham told *The Newark Advertiser*, 'It is now well known that there are such animals living in the wild. The problem is no-one sees them for long enough to confirm the sightings.'

The Newark Advertiser also reported the comments of Dr Peter Davies, zoologist and senior lecturer at Nottingham University. He said it is possible for a panther to be living wild in the UK, that such a cat could be preying on small deer, rabbits and other native species, and that it could pose a threat to farm animals such as poultry and lambs. Dr Davies added that he had not heard of a wild big cat attacking a person in the UK.

I appealed in the local press for more witnesses to come forward. Mrs June Hornby of Newark wrote to me, obviously relieved to unburden herself of a worrying memory: 'Regarding your letter in *The Newark Advertiser* about the 'large cats' I wonder if you might find the following interesting. I would like to say at the outset, I am tee total so I didn't see any of this through the bottom of a glass.

'Some four years ago (circa 1995) after the yearly barbecue my husband and I throw, we had cleared up with the help of our two friends who were staying with us for the weekend. It was around 2.45 am and I had decided, after the other three went to bed, to have a much longed for cup of tea and a few minutes' peace and quiet. I finished the tea and before retiring to bed pulled back the bedroom curtains a fraction (the room overlooks the road) and outside the shop which is opposite our house there is a large green council litterbin. To my surprise I saw what I thought was someone leaning against the bin. I was about to open the window and call out asking if they were OK when the 'someone' moved and to my horror, or surprise really, I saw what I know to be a large black cat.

'Its tail was extremely long and rope-like and it swished on the ground as it walked away. It went as far as the corner of the road, which leads to the Harvey Avenue estate, and stopped and turned. I moved the curtains further back and it saw the movement and turned its head towards me. The eyes were glowing in the streetlight and it was quite beautiful. Something must have startled it then, because it bounded away towards the small copse/wood at the end of the estate towards what used to be the equestrian centre.

'I was loath to mention this to anybody for fear of ridicule; however, I did. The following morning I was in the shop, a few people were there and they heard me mention it to Mr Lunn the proprietor. He actually believed me, although I did come in for some mickey taking – you know the kind of thing, "who had too much to drink last night" etc. However, Mr Lunn assured them that I never ever drank. We exchanged a few more pleasantries and I left the shop.

'As I was about to cross the road, I was stopped by an elderly gentleman who said, "I am so glad somebody else has seen it. I can't sleep too well now, so in the early hours, about 3 or 4 am, I take my old Labrador for a walk as far as Stapleford Woods and last week when I was there my dog suddenly stopped and began to growl. I held on to his collar thinking it must be a badger or fox, when suddenly from out of the undergrowth appeared this large black cat. I was too frightened to move and held on to my dog for grim death just in case he decided to have a go. However, within seconds the animal had gone. It was close enough for me to smell its musky odour. I told my family and they said I must be getting old and dotty, but I know what I saw. I'm just glad somebody else has seen it."

'I hope the foregoing has been of interest to you. As to whether I believed before this happened that big cats were around, well, I did and I didn't, but I am now firmly convinced big cats *are* around, possibly having been released from some private collection. Wishing you success in your venture. Mrs June Hornby.'

Could big cats really be roaming free? What kind of animals are they? Based on the eyewitness reports researchers have suggested the leopard, the puma and the lynx as possible suspects.

The natural habitat of black leopards (the so-called 'black panthers') is humid rain forest. Leopards can go without water by obtaining moisture from their prey and will eat anything from dung beetles to deer. Researchers have found that male leopards killed every three days on average, and females with cubs every 1½ days. So a half a dozen rabbits, taken every other day could sustain a leopard.

The next suspect, the lynx, has been kept as an exotic pet and bred in fur farms in the U.K. Lynxes could have been released into the wild following the 1976 Dangerous Animal Act. They are stout-bodied, 65 to 130 cm in length, dark grey in colour with a greyish-white belly, thick, soft fur, and stubby tails. Lynxes feed chiefly on rabbits and hares and could live wild in the U.K. given enough range and prey. It is certainly suited to our climate. However, the mystery big cat is described as black in colour and having a long tail.

The mountain lion, *aka* the puma or cougar, is found from snowy British Columbia to the southern tip of South America. This is a large, solitary animal, ranging in size from 100 to 170 pounds and from five to eight feet in length, including the tail. It avoids open grasslands, agricultural areas and people. Could this animal survive in the overcrowded British Isles?

The frequency and distribution of sightings does suggest that some sort of big cat may be breeding successfully in the UK. These animals may have escaped from private collections or been deliberately released by wholly irresponsible people. There is some physical evidence – blurred video tapes, photographs, plaster casts of footprints, and carcasses of prey animals – so it would seem that the creatures are not of supernatural orgin as ancient folklore suggests. But why haven't any of these animals been run over on our busy roads, or shot or trapped by a game keeper? The big black cat mystery remains.

MURDER BY SPOUSE

On average, two women per week are killed in England and Wales by their partners or ex-partners. Forty-five per cent of UK female homicide victims are killed by current or former male partners, compared with 8% of male victims (Criminal Statistics (1992) Home Office). Domestic violence is one of the most common crimes and one of the most difficult to police. Almost half (44%) of all incidents reported by women are domestic violence incidents (British Crime Survey 1996, Home Office). However, only one out of three crimes of this nature resulting in injury are reported (British Crime Survey, 1996). Studies show that women are at greatest risk of homicide at the point of separation or after leaving a violent partner (Daly & Wilson (1998) *Homicide*, Aldane Gruyter). The murder of Vicki Older tragically conforms to known patterns of domestic homicides.

One June night in 1999 40-year-old Gary Eyres walked from his home in Forster Road, Radford to Strelley carrying a pickaxe handle and a knife with a 18 cm blade. He was on his way to see his ex-partner, 30-year-old Vicki Older. Eyres had been drinking heavily all that day.

Eyres had met Vicki in 1992 and they had a daughter together. Vicki already had a daughter from a previous relationship and the four lived together as a family. The relationship broke up in 1996. Vicki Older was a woman living in fear, who had suffered years of threats and harassment from Gary Eyres. The harassment intensified, until Vicki believed Eyres was stalking her. When he arrived at Mrs Older's home in Cranwell Road, Strelley, she refused to let him in and hid inside the house with her two young daughters. Gary Eyres used the pickaxe handle to smash his way into her home before stabbing her nineteen times in the chest and back.

Vicki Older had endured three years of torment at the hands of Gary Eyres. Despite their relationship breaking up Eyres refused to let go. Said her mother, Jean Freeman, 'I remember one afternoon when she rang from a local shop in a real state. She had nipped out to buy a few things and had seen him hanging around. She refused to leave the shop and I had to go and collect her. He just wouldn't leave her alone.'

When Vicki and the two girls moved into the house in Cranwell Road, Eyres continued to harass them. Perhaps as a means to obtain copies of the keys, he offered to put locks on the door of Vicki's new home. The offer was declined. At this time he seemed to think he and Vicki could be reconciled and that he would move into the house with them. Eyres' drinking was becoming uncontrollable. He became more obsessive about Vicki and his daughter and wouldn't give up, even when Vicki met someone else. Tensions grew steadily between him, Vicki and her new boyfriend.

In the years after his relationship with Vicki Older broke down, Eyres became an alcoholic, on an emotional roller coaster, careering between worsening episodes of depression and manic drinking binges. He continued to torment Vicki to such an extent that she started to keep a logbook of incidents. Over a three-year period Vicki made dozens of entries. The police became involved more and more frequently but there was little they could do to resolve the situation.

In the months before the attack, Eyres had become increasingly frustrated over his access to his daughter, which was limited and supervised, by court order. There was at least one occasion when his daughter was reluctant to be with Eyres for an arranged visit. Eyres came to believe that Vicki and her family were conspiring to keep him away from his daughter. He became more sinister and began to make serious threats. Bullets were pushed through Vicki's letter-box and her boyfriend's car was repeatedly vandalised. Despite their best efforts police couldn't prove that Eyres was responsible.

The threats became more specific and more frightening, Eyres threatened to burn Vicki's house down and to kill her. The police warned Eyres off several times but to no avail. With access rights Eyres could still maintain his supervised contact sessions with his daughter, which he used as a way of maintaining his campaign of fear against Vicki. During one such visit, just weeks before the killing, Eyres threatened Vicki's father with the chilling words, 'Your daugher has taken my daughter so I am going to take your daughter – she's dead.'

Neighbours in Cranwell Road heard Eyres hit the front window of Mrs Older's house three times and came out of their houses to investigate. They saw Vicki's children screaming for help from an upper window. Eyres smashed the window and dived through head first, chasing Vicki Older upstairs. Eyres cornered Vicki in her bedroom and killed her. Moments later neighbours saw a man covered in blood walking from the scene holding a knife and called the police. Police officers raced to Cranwell Road; when they arrived Vicki was still alive and was able to tell them it was Eyres who had stabbed her. Despite the desperate first aid efforts of officers on the scene Vicki was fatally wounded and was pronounced dead a short time later.

With a name and a description police began to look for Eyres. They didn't have to look far. Eyres had cut his hand after smashing through the window and police followed the trail of blood. A few minutes later he was arrested by Sgt. William Chell. At this point Eyres seemed to have lost his mind. He asked Sgt. Chell, 'Is she dead?' Then Eyres look up to the sky and said, 'I hope she's up there.' The murder weapon was found outside the Strelley Social Club. The arresting officers found that Eyres was in no fit state to be interviewed when taken into custody; he couldn't even remember his age or address.

The awful conclusion of this campaign of terror came on that June night when he stabbed Vicki nineteen times and left her two girls motherless.

At his trial there was no question as to whether Gary Eyres had killed Vicki Older; it was his state of mind at the time that was at issue. In his defence Eyres denied murder on the grounds of diminished responsibility. In the weeks before he killed Vicki, Eyres had made a number of threats to take his own life and repeated these threats after his arrest. Giving evidence he told the court he was angry with his ex-girlfriend after she refused to give him access to their five-year-old daughter. Eyres described how he had been drinking all day and went to Vicki's home in Cranwell Road

Gary Eyres stabbed his ex-partner 19 times after smashing his way into her home with a pick-axe handle.

with the intention of 'speaking' to her.

John Milmo, QC, prosecuting, asked why he had gone to Mrs Older's house armed with a pickaxe handle and a knife: 'Did you honestly expect her to be reasonable, and give you access rights to your daughter, after you had just smashed your way into her home?' he said. 'Did it not occur to you to knock on the door? The truth is you had been planning this for some time and went to her house with the sole intention of killing her'. Eyres claimed he only meant to frighten Vicki with the knife and lost his temper after she made a remark to him. He told the court, 'I just wanted to frighten her, I had no intention of killing her. I can remember stabbing her three times, but cannot remember anything after that. It was terrible. I just couldn't cope with anything at all. I just wanted to see my daughter.'

The jury heard differing opinions from psychiatrists as to whether Eyres was seriously mentally ill, or depressed and still in control of his actions. Dr Diana Tamlyn, a consultant psychiatrist at Rampton Hospital, said Gary Eyres was not suffering from a delusional disorder when he stabbed Vicki Older nineteen times. Her evidence followed an earlier medical witness who had concluded that Eyres was mentally ill. Dr Tamlyn agreed that he was moderately depressed but thought that this alone did not explain why he took Mrs Older's life. Dr Tamlyn was of the opinion that the alcohol had played a part in the attack. Giving evidence Det Supt Kevin Flint said, 'In interview, Eyres claimed to have selective memory of the incident but he had clearly gone equipped with a weapon and something with which to break the window. The killing is tragic in a number of ways. He has killed the mother of two children. He has to live with that for the rest of his life.'

The jury of three women and nine men spent a day and a half weighing up the evidence. They couldn't agree on the central issues of the case and failed to reach a verdict. The judge, Mr Justice Morland, discharged them and called counsel into chambers to resolve the issues that had been raised during the trial, chiefly that of Eyres' mental condition at the time he killed Vicki Older. Prosecuting Counsel John Milmo, QC, was willing to accept the plea to manslaughter by diminished responsibility, but only after discussions with the police and Vicki's family. Defence counsel, Charles Wide, QC, said his client's illness meant he still presented a risk and asked the judge to detain him under the Mental Health Act. Passing sentence Mr Justice Morland told Eyres: 'You are vulnerable to relapses for the foreseeable future and there is a significant risk you may not make a recovery. You remain a potential danger to the public at large and in particular to the family of the deceased and for those reasons I propose to detain you for an unlimited time in a secure hospital. You will not be able to leave this hospital and it may be you will be there for many years.' Eyres will be detained for an unlimited period in a secure hospital.

LIKE AN EXECUTION

Police described the killing of Janet McGhee as more like an execution than a domestic murder. Her estranged husband, Thomas McGhee, a former college lecturer, had meticulously planned the killing and carefully prepared his escape. Described as a highly intelligent man to the point of being cunning, Thomas McGhee displayed traits that suggest he may have had some kind of compulsive obsessive disorder. During their four year stormy marriage McGhee would plan even the simplest of activities down to the smallest detail; he was a domineering control freak. His treatment of Janet during their marriage was described as brutal. He would not let her do anything without his supervision, when they were together he would not let her talk to anyone and he would not let her have any friends. When Janet finally made a new life for herself Thomas McGhee hunted her down and killed her, shooting her twice through the glass door of a friend's home where she had desperately sought sanctuary.

Janet had known Thomas McGhee for over 30 years. They had been sweethearts in the early 1970s and had planned to marry. However, they split up and Janet met and married Jeff Edwards, from Eastwood. Jeff and Janet were married for 24 years before amicably divorcing. Some time later Janet again met up with Thomas McGhee. After a brief courtship, they married and move to Hinckley, Leicestershire in 1990. Their first year of marriage seemed normal and the

Thomas McGee
meticulously planned
the killing of his wife.

couple had a daughter together. Then the dark side of
Thomas's character began to assert itself and soon Janet's life
became a living hell. Eventually her family had to rescue her
from the domineering bully who was her husband. For
nearly two months Janet's family kept her in hiding, so
afraid were they of Thomas McGhee. Following a court
injunction Janet got possession of a house in Eastwood and
began to make a new life for herself.

Janet moved from Eastwood to Kimberley and found
herself living close to some old friends. Karen and Brian
Gough had known Janet for 22 years but had lost contact
when she married Thomas McGhee. Janet had known that
the Goughs haboured strong misgivings about McGhee so
she hadn't told them when she married him and went to
Leicestershire. With her friends once more the details of her

awful time with McGhee came out. She told of how she had gone to live in a refuge to escape McGhee's obsessive control over her, of the abuse she had suffered, of how McGhee had begun a hate campaign against her in Kimberley, spreading lies and malicious gossip, and how she now feared for her life.

Meanwhile Thomas McGhee was planning to kill his wife. He hired a second car from a firm in Derbyshire, which he parked in a quiet lane three miles from Janet's home. In his own white Astra he placed a shotgun, cartridges and hack-saw. McGhee's daughter was staying with him that weekend in Hinckley. It was arranged that he would take her back to Janet's home in Eastwood Road, Kimberley. Instead he took the child to his relatives, telling them to look after her and handing over £100 in cash. Then he set off for Kimberley. At some point he used the hack-saw on the gun to create the murderous 'sawn-off' weapon favoured by gangsters and assassins for close-in work.

On the bitterly cold evening of Monday 1st December, 1996 McGhee cornered Janet at her home. Janet had lived in mortal fear of McGhee for years and now he had failed to bring her daughter home. A heated argument ensued, Janet fled to the Goughs' house, pursued by McGhee. The Goughs, blissfully unaware of the drama about to engulf them, were busy making food for a children's party. At what point McGhee brandished the gun is unclear. He may have had it concealed on his person or he may have retrieved it from his car. What is known is that Janet barely had time to get inside the Goughs' house and attempt to lock the door before the first shot shattered the glass.

As she burst through the front door screaming that McGhee had a gun, the key fell from the lock to the floor. McGhee could see his wife's blurred image through the frosted glass frantically trying to lock the door. As McGhee blasted her with the sawn off, Brian Gough was already running to the door. Seeing the danger he dropped to the floor and pushed the door closed with his feet, while Janet, bleeding from the shotgun wound, managed to get up into a sitting position at the bottom of the stairs. Still on the floor Brian Gough watched as the twin barrels of the gun were poked through the gaping hole in the door and a second shot was fired, hitting Janet in the chest. The blast deafened him as he shouted desperately to his son, Nick, to call the police. Brian feared his whole family would be killed. It seemed an eternity before the sawn off shotgun was pulled back through the shattered door.

Janet lay slumped on the floor, her eyes open but unseeing. The Goughs tried to give Janet first aid but there was nothing they could do to save her. Thomas McGhee was seen calmly walking away to his Astra. There was no doubt in the mind of Brian Gough that if he hadn't pushed the door shut with his feet McGhee would have got into the house and begun firing indiscriminately. Police raced to the scene and were alerted by witnesses that McGhee, stilled armed, had made threats to kill members of Janet's family.

Armed officers sped to the family's isolated farm a few miles from the murder scene. McGhee enacted his escape plan, dumped his car and picked up the get away hire car. He remained at large, so police tried to trap him by taking members of Janet's family to a secret location and occupying their house with armed police. But McGhee didn't show up. When his Astra was found in Church Road, Watnall, the sawn-off barrels of a shotgun, a hacksaw and two spent shotgun cartridges were found. They were heavy gauge shot, known as Goose Shot.

A large-scale hunt for McGhee using dogs and mounted officers was begun. Four days after the murder McGhee was seen in a car by a young girl. Her suspicions aroused, she told her father, who called the police. An armed response team was called and McGhee was arrested without incident.

At his trial Thomas McGhee claimed he was suffering from a depressive illness. Defence barrister Edward Rees,

QC, offered a plea of guilty of manslaughter on the grounds of diminished responsibility. However, senior police officers involved in the case drew attention to the way McGhee had planned the killing down to the last detail. In the opinion of police this was not a domestic murder committed in the heat of the moment, it was more like a cold-blooded execution. In evidence police pointed out that McGhee, after shooting Janet twice, had coolly walked back to his car and made good his escape.

The jury of ten men and two women took two and a half hours to reach their unanimous verdict, guilty of murder. They rejected the defence claim that at the time of the killing McGhee was suffering from a depressive illness. In his closing remarks the trial judge, Mr Justice Ognall, told McGhee, 'In a determined and pre-meditated fashion you took the life of your wife in the most brutal circumstances.' Standing in the dock McGhee seemed indifferent. He was sentenced to life imprisonment.

As a codicil to the McGhee case, a similar shooting occurred the following year. On 8th October 1997, Wayne Topps, estranged from his girlfriend Alijca Pieniazek, went to her family home in Littlegreen Road, Woodthorpe, armed with a loaded handgun.

Topps shot Alijca's 64-year-old mother, Eugenia Pieniazek, twice through a glass door. Police arrived minutes later and Topps opened fire on them. PC Alan Booth was hit in the shoulder but struggled with the gunman and effected the arrest with his colleague PC Ringer. PC Booth didn't realise he had been shot until he felt pain in his neck and shoulder after the arrest.

Inside the house Eugenia Pieniazak was seriously wounded. One bullet had passed straight through her lungs narrowly missing the aorta, the main artery from the heart. The second bullet passed through her neck and jaw before lodging half an inch from her spinal cord. Two major operations and four weeks in intensive care saved her life.

Surgeons found it too dangerous to remove the bullet next to her spinal cord and had to leave it there.

Although he was wearing a stab-proof vest the bullet hit PC Booth in an unprotected area of the shoulder. He was the first Nottinghamshire police officer to be shot on duty since 1927, when three bullets hit PC Edward Dainty as he attempted to arrest Edgar William Smith in Newark Road, Farndon. PC Dainty managed to write down part of Smith's car registration and he was later tracked down and gaoled for life.

PC Booth and PC Ringer acted in the finest traditions of the police force as they faced the gunman. If they hadn't acted so selflessly, Topps would have had the opportunity to kill the whole Pieniazek family. As it was, it was a miracle Topps didn't have two deaths on his hands. PC Booth and PC Ringer were both given bravery awards. For attempted murder Topps, from Bulwell, was given two life sentences at Nottingham Crown Court in December 1998. Mr Justice Poole recommended that Topps should serve a minimum of ten years in gaol before he is considered for parole.

THE CHILWELL EXPLOSION MYSTERY

1918 was the terrible last year of World War I and to some it must have seemed like the end of the world. By then every family in Britain had lost someone in the war and yet the last German offensives had pushed the front lines back. July 1918 saw an influenza outbreak which became one the worst pandemics in history, claiming an estimated 21 million lives worldwide before it abated in November. The world was glutted with violence and death. Coming as it did at the end of four years of carnage the Chilwell Explosion was one more horror to be endured in a world numbed by horror.

At about 8 pm on 1st July 1918 the Chilwell Shell Filling factory near Nottingham was ripped apart by a massive blast. Nearly eight tons of high explosives went up. The explosion was so great that it was heard in the Vale of Belvoir some 15 miles away. Buildings were shaken as though in an earthquake and windows were blown out as far away as Long Eaton, 2 miles away. Farm workers in fields at Bramcote saw twisted metal blown into the air and tumble to the ground. The destruction was on a huge scale. One hundred and forty four people were killed, 25 of them women, and a further 250 people were injured. Only fourteen of the bodies were identifiable; the remaining 120 were buried in a mass grave in Attenborough village churchyard.

Mystery surrounds this disaster, which was responsible

for the greatest loss of life ever suffered in a single explosion in Britain. And there may have been more than just 'The Fog of War' covering up the cause. The factory was built by Lord Chetwynd in 1916; in the first two years of operations there were 19 minor explosions. According to Lord Chetwynd many of them were caused by deliberate tampering. From the outset Lord Chetwynd believed that the 1918 disaster was the result of sabotage. If he was right and the fact had been made public, the effect on the morale of the nation would have been dire. The war effort was at a crucial stage; political and social tensions were at bursting point; if a worker at the factory had committed murder on this scale the outrage of the nation could have had far reaching consequences. The report from the inquiry into the explosion was not published, nor was it shown to Lord Chetwynd. Could government officials have acted to contain this incident and maintain production at all costs? Did the men from the ministry really allow a mass murderer to escape justice for the sake of the war effort? Who was ultimately responsible for the appalling loss of life?

Britain in July 1918 was a very different place from Britain in 1914. The war caused unprecedented social upheavels, forcing huge numbers of women into the work force. For the first time women were working in factories doing the same physically and technically demanding work as the men. Though they weren't given equal pay, women workers were seen as a threat by some male workers. At the Chilwell factory the electricians had tried to strike, unhappy about women doing 'their' jobs.

All the shells used in the Battle of the Somme came from Chilwell and 60% of all shells used in World War I were filled at the factory. Lottie Wiggins started work at Chilwell in April 1916. Along with eight other girls she was taken to the Filled Shells Store: 'My first impression of that store was sheer fright, rows and rows of 8 inch, 6 inch and 9 inch shells, not forgetting the 12 inch, which reached up to my

Chilwell – the aftermath of the explosion on 4th July 1918.

waist and higher. I hardly dared walk near them but had to overcome this feeling. As I remember it there were fifteen bays in the store . . . We were on eight-hour shifts at first but this changed to twelve hours, this meant two shifts instead of three. Twelve hours Monday to Saturday then it changed to eighteen hours, going on duty at 6 o'clock Saturday evening and working to 2 o'clock Sunday afternoon when the opposite shift would take over . . . No one would work those long hours today . . . this was war and everyone was out to get results. Soon weekly output of filled shells reached 13,000, which required 900 tons of Amatol.'

A Factory Inspector's Report gives us some sense of the scale of operations at Chilwell: 'This Great Store, which covers seven acres of ground, is designed to hold a stock of 50,000 shells. Working at full pressure the operatives in this store can unload from the railway wagons, clean, paint, examine and reload in wagons for dispatch to the Filling Departments up to 40,000 shells in 24 hours . . .'

By the summer of 1918 the factory employed nearly 10,000 people, 4,000 of them women. The canteen served 30,000 meals every day. Production was reaching its peak with the record for daily production being set on 15th June when 46,725 shells were filled in a 24-hour period.

The explosion occurred two years to the day after the slaughter on the Somme began. Gladys Roper, a munitions worker, remembered that fateful moment when the factory exploded: '. . . there was a series of almighty blasts, the lights went out for a few seconds and then on again. Everyone tried to make for the safety barriers but it seemed the whole place was falling apart.'

The Mixing House, TNT Mill, and TNT stores were completely destroyed along with the police station, fire station, No. 1 Motor Garage, No. 1 Canteen and other minor buildings. The Ammonium Nitrate House and crusher were left standing but badly damaged. The Power House, hospital, nurses' bungalow and laboratory were also seriously damaged. Every window in the factory was shattered.

Rebecca Roper, another munitions worker, recalled, '. . . utter devastation, there were people running around with the most terrible head injuries and shattered limbs.'

Crane operator Barretta Wood remembered, 'I was just passing half an orange to Sadie Adams and there was this tremendous bang and everything seemed to disappear including the shells suspended from my crane. I slid down the rope and was picked up off the floor by a man who put his left arm around me and carried me out of the shed, his right arm had been blown clean off and both of us were covered in blood.'

Alma Vaughan was shopping in Chilwell when the explosion happened; 'I had just left a shop when suddenly there was a shattering noise, a huge volume of black smoke filled the sky, the shop window splintered over me, and I heard screams of the people around me shouting "the

Women at the munitions factory were doing the same physically and technically demanding work as the men.

factory has gone". My first reaction was terror, and then the thought of what had happened to my family. I cycled back to the depot in a hysterical state and when I reached the factory gate I was prevented from entering and was told our home was destroyed and maybe my family also. I saw horrible sights . . .'

Just 11-years-old at the time, Mrs Kate Abdy was an eye witness. 'I raced towards the works after hearing the huge bang and saw the awful sight of debris hanging in the golden sky, so clear that the bodies of those unfortunate people seemed to be suspended for some time, spread-eagled, before slowly coming earthwards.'

A government official visiting the day after the blast said, 'The destruction reminded me of places I saw on the Somme and Flanders. The difference being that there the destruction was the work of months of bambardment but at Chilwell it was the work of a moment.'

Production had to continue. Two days later, on Wednesday 3rd July, shell filling restarted; by the following day 7,800 shells had been filled. In *The Times* newspaper of 9th July Mr F G Kellaway, MP, was quoted as saying, 'One can judge the courage of that great staff when he knows that the next morning out of 7,000 men and women all but twelve put in an appearance and were ready to commence work again.'

The Home Office Enquiry Committee was convened on 8th July 1918 under the Chairmanship of Sir Ernley Blackwell. Government officials spent only two days at the site. The Committee's report was marked 'SECRET' and presented on 7th August – less than a month after the explosion. Scotland Yard also carried out an investigation. Inspector Cornish was on the scene before the government team and the official report relies heavily on witness statements taken by the Inspector.

Lord Chetwynd, as Managing Director of the factory, made a lengthy statement to both Inspector Cornish and the government officials. Lord Chetwynd believed that the explosion occurred on the ground floor of the Mixing House and was an act of sabotage involving a group of electricians . . . 'men of rabid socialist tendencies', as he had described them in a letter about a strike at the factory to Mr C R Duggan at the Ministry of Munitions. Further to this Lord Chetwynd said in his statement to Inspector Cornish, 'It must be admitted that it is at least a remarkable coincidence that one of those men, by name Gott, should have been one of the day shift electricians in the Mills on 1st July, taking the place of man named Bradshaw, who should have been on duty but was said to be away ill . . . Another curious coincidence is the fact that both the two electricians on duty on the night of 1st July, Seabrook and Mann, were in the sub-station of the Ammonium Nitrate Mill when the explosion took place. They should have been attending to their duties in the Mills. The position in which they were when the explosion took place was probably the safest position in the Mills or in any of the Mill buildings . . . In my opinion there would have been no difficulty in the way of a clever engineer with electrical knowledge putting a small time detonator in one of the tubs (on the ground floor of the Mixing House) as long as he was prepared to take the risk of being seen putting it in . . .'

Mr J A Cook, a powder controller, told the enquiry team he had seen three men looking into No.1 Mixer, which was unusual, especially when it was being filled. One of the men, a conveyor attendant, explained that they had been looking for a piece of metal which was missing from the conveyor. Mr Cook concluded that the missing piece must have been bigger than a nut or bolt or the conveyor attendant wouldn't have missed it. Five minutes after Mr Cook left the Mixing House the explosion ripped the factory apart.

However, some witness statments suggest the disaster was an industrial accident. John Weston was a charge hand in the Powder Galleries: 'So far as I know none of the men suspect foul play in connection with this explosion, neither do I. The general opinion is that the explosion is due to overheating of the machinery.' Walter Smith, a Mixing House worker said, '. . . in my opinion the machinery had been overrun for some weeks, it is caused through one shift trying to turn out more powder than the other.'

Harry Stevenson, also a Mixing House worker: 'I think it quite possible a hot bearing could be the cause of the explosion'.

Inspector Cornish returned to Scotland Yard on 17th July, his investigations complete. He gave his report to the Enquiry Committee at the Home Office on 18th July. Inspector Cornish concluded, 'To me the cause of the explosion is obscure. There is no evidence whatever of foul play or of an accident and none will be forthcoming unless, if it is foul play, the guilty party makes some admission, because everyone who could have thrown any light on the matter has been seen and everything of importance in this direction obtained from them. I regret that I cannot make the matter more clear, but in the absence of one iota of evidence it is impossible for me to determine the case . . .'

The Home Office Enquiry produced its report on 7th August, incredibly quickly for any government enquiry. It stated that the explosion could have only two possible causes: 1) Malicious act. 2) Accident to or in connection with machinery. The report considered that the cause was probably a piece of metal from the conveyor falling into No.1 Mixer in the Mixing House. However, the report also says, 'For the reasons given in this report, the possibility of enemy sabotage or action of a disaffected worker having caused the explosion, cannot be disregarded.'

The possibility of sabotage does not appear to have been very thoroughly pursued. It is known that German intelligence operatives tried to bomb the factory as it was being built in January 1916. The enquiry committee did deal in depth with Lord Chetwynd's theory concerning the role of Gott and the two other electricians, who were at a safe distance when the explosion occurred. They found it was quite normal for the electricians to be where they were. Gott didn't report into work after the explosion; nor did Inspector Cornish or the enquiry investigators question him. Gott was transferred to another munitions factory in Scotland within three days of the explosion. He seems to have disappeared after that. Only one of the 'rabid socialists' named by Lord Chetwynd was interviewed. Henry Watson, an electrician's mate, was on duty on the day before the blast. Inspector Cornish had found that Watson had avoided military service before being declared medically unfit in 1917 and had had some twelve different jobs before coming to Chilwell six months prior to the explosion. Investigation into his background went no further.

The enquiry concluded that most likely cause seemed to be machine failure, overloading or suspect production methods. However, the enquiry report states 'We have no specific recommendations to make, but in view of this accident the construction and method of working in factories in which shells are filled with Amatol or similar explosives will no doubt be examined in the light of our Report.' One hundred and forty-four dead and 250 injured and no recommendations were made – curious to say the least.

The report was careful not to suggest design faults in the production process or any degree of mismanagament, which would have been the ultimate responsibility of Lord Chetwynd himself. If practices in the factory had been to blame, the public outcry at the appalling injuries and loss of life suffered would have been highly damaging to the Ministry of Munitions. Methods in use at Chilwell were common to other munitions factories and the Ministry had enough problems recruiting munitions workers as it was.

The Ministry of Munitions' report has been unearthed in the Public Records Office at Kew, but studying the report still leaves questions unanswered. Was this mass murder by sabotage? If so, by whom? A disaffected worker? Was someone using the anniversary of the Battle of the Somme to make a grotesque point about the quality of the shells? – one reason given for the enormous casualties on the first day of the Somme is the failure of the barrage to wipe out the German lines. Why were dud shells found in the wreckage of the factory? Or was it a case of workers and machinery being overworked for the sake of output, resulting in the sacrifice of the lives of 144 people? At the site of the explosion, inside what is now the Chetwynd Barracks, the memorial to those who died is still respectfully maintained.

KIDNAP, MURDER AND THE PSYCHIC DETECTIVE

On Tuesday, 5th January 1937, just after 4 pm, ten-year-old Mona Tinsley left her school in Guildhall Street, Newark to walk home as usual to Thoresby Avenue. She never arrived. Her distraught parents searched the streets and called at homes of friends and family in the area looking for Mona. At 9 pm her father reported her to the police as missing.

Harry Barnes, the Chief Constable for Newark, ordered an immediate search. Police checked outhouses, gardens and sheds. They walked the banks of the river Trent and began house to house inquiries. Mona had been seen that evening in the company of a man; she was later seen at Newark bus station with the same man; then reports came in of her being seen after that at Retford. From there the trail went cold – all trace of Mona Tinsley vanished.

Police were quickly able to establish the identity of the man seen with the missing child. Mrs Anne Hird, a neighbour of the Tinsleys', contacted the police to report that she had seen a man waiting outside Mona's school at around 4 pm. Mrs Hird recognised the man as Frederick Nodder, who used to lodge with the Tinsleys. Further inquiries revealed that a girl of about Mona's age had been seen in the garden of Nodder's house at Smeath Lane, Hayton, near Retford. Nodder was arrested and taken into police custody for questioning.

At first Nodder denied being in Newark that day or being

with the child. However, he did admit to knowing the girl. In 1935 Nodder had had lodgings with Mrs Tinsley at 11 Thoresby Avenue, Newark. He made himself popular with the Tinsleys' children, who knew him as 'Uncle Fred'. He didn't stay with the Tinsleys' long, being asked to leave Thoresby Avenue after only a few weeks. Contemporary descriptions show Nodder as an ugly, brutish drunk who had difficulty in holding down a job. Changing his name to Hudson, he moved to a house named 'Peacehaven' near to Hayton, Retford.

Confronted with witness statements linking him with the missing child on the day in question Nodder changed his story. According to his statement he had been asked by the child to take her to Sheffield to visit her aunt and baby cousin; she had then attempted to persuade him to take her to Retford, from where she could get another bus to Sheffield. As it was a winter's afternoon and getting dark Nodder suggested that the child spend the night at 'Peacehaven'. He claimed that the next day he had taken Mona from Retford to Worksop on the bus, given her two shillings for her fare and put her on another bus for Sheffield. As convoluted as it sounds, Nodder stuck to his story.

The police conducted an exhaustive search aided by some 900 volunteers. They made a thorough search of 'Peacehaven', they dragged the Chesterfield Canal and the River Idle and they searched the countryside for miles around. There was no sign of the child. Nodder was charged with abduction. In custody, and irrefutably linked with Mona's disappearance, Nodder callously denied all knowledge of the girl's fate.

The case of the missing child caught the imagination of the popular press and the disappearance of Mona Tinsley became national news. It was at this time that Douglas Sladen, a friend of the famous medium Estelle Roberts, contacted Newark police offering help in tracing Mona.

Estelle Roberts was described as 'one of the world's greatest mediums and the possessor of nearly every psychic faculty' by Maurice Barbanell in his book *This is Spiritualism*. She had established a wide reputation during the 1920s and '30s. However, at first, the police were reluctant to accept her help.

Estelle Roberts claimed that in mid January she had been visited by the dead girl's spirit. The police were intrigued; no body had as yet been found and this was still officially a missing persons case. Estelle Roberts was able to persuade the chief constable that she could help the police with the case if she could have one of Mona's dresses to hold as an aid to Red Cloud, her Red Indian spirit guide. As banal as this sounds, the Chief Constable agreed. Estelle wrote later, "As I took it from its wrapping . . . I knew at once that Mona was

Estelle Roberts – 'one of the world's greatest mediums and the possessor of nearly every psychic faculty'.

dead. Just then, my old dog, who had been sleeping, suddenly leapt to his feet and began to career madly around the room." (Estelle Roberts, *Forty Years A Medium* (London: Herbert Jenkin, 1959, p.71).

Subsequently, Estelle claimed the she spoke with Mona through Red Cloud, the dead girl describing how she had been taken to a small house and strangled. Estelle Roberts gave the police details of Nodder's house and described the surrounding area to them. Further to this she said she was sure she knew where the child's body had been taken. The police were impressed. Estelle suggested that further psychic revelations could be made if she were to visit the crime scene. This was arranged. After travelling by train to Newark, Estelle was met by police with a car. They drove the medium

Red Cloud, or Makhpiya Luta, 1822–1909, head chief of the Oglala Lakota, a Sioux Indian people.

to Hayton. Once in the locality Estelle was able to direct them to Smeath Lane and, from the car, recognize the house where the murder had taken place, as she claimed Mona had described it to her. On entering the house Estelle said she felt the child's presence.

Next, Estelle Roberts spoke to Mona's parents. Aided by her spirit guide, Red Cloud, she was able to describe how Mona had been assaulted and murdered. Estelle said at the time that she didn't enjoy dealing with such cases because of the strain it placed on her; she was nevertheless willing to help bereaved people. From the house Estelle led police across the Canal Bridge and into nearby fields. Here Red Cloud lost the trail but Estelle insisted that a river lay some way ahead, into which the body had been dumped. The River Idle was indeed beyond the fields. Police had already dragged the river once and, as it was now in flood, due to the January rains, a further search was suspended.

On a sunny afternoon in June 1937 Walter Marshall was rowing his family along the river. He noticed something in the water and got nearer to investigate. He was horrified to see a child's body lodged in the reeds and mud. Gaining the bank, Mr Marshall sent his son for the police. Walter Marshall helped the officer attending, PC Sheridan, to drag the body onto the bank. She was dressed as she had been on the day she disappeared; only her coat and one boot were missing. Mr Tinsley formally identified the body as Mona's. The post mortem revealed that she had been strangled with a ligature. The body was too decomposed to reveal whether she had been sexually assaulted. Frederick Nodder was then charged with her murder and brought before the Nottingham Assizes on 22nd November. He was found guilty and sentenced to death. His hanging took place at Lincoln Prison on 30th December 1937.

The spiritualist community made much of Estelle Roberts' involvement in the Mona Tinsley case at the time. But did Estelle's psychic revelations add anything new to the police

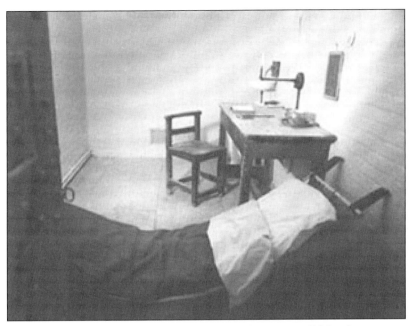

Awaiting execution, Nodder spent his last days in a cell like this at Lincoln prison.

investigation at all?

Looking back at the revelations Estelle made there seems to be little about them that was supernatural. All her claims could have been arrived at by making educated guesses and reading the press reports at the time. As to directing the police to the house, couldn't a previous scrutiny of a street map or directions from a third party have provided the details without Red Cloud's assistance? But if Estelle Roberts was faking it, how was she able to gain the attention of senior police officers?

Many people claim to be psychic. Palm readers and astrologers claim that they look into the future to help solve personal problems. Mediums claim to communicate with the dead. However, research (Kocsis, 1998; Pinnozoto, 1987) has established that psychics are no more accurate than a control group simply making guesses. But the police have a duty to follow up every lead, so if a psychic offers convincing sounding information they must be included in the investigation. This aspect of the application of psychic abilities has been the focus of serious academic research, research that has come up with the conclusion that some psychics do cheat. Whether they do more harm than good when dealing with grieving relatives is a moot point. However, when the *faux* psychic becomes involved to the extent that they hamper police work, or divert precious time and resources, their use becomes a matter of importance.

Research has shown that people tend to interpret ambiguous information to 'fit' their own personal agendas (Sundberg, 1955; Hyman, 1981). This has been termed the 'fallacy of personal validation' (Forer, 1949). Some psychics exploit this tendency by using a technique called 'cold reading'.

Cold reading involves giving out lots of vague information and educated guesses to a client in order to make it seem that more information has been given than actually has. Objective analysis of consultations with psychics reveals that the client is manipulated into 'co-authoring' the revelations made by the psychic. The unwary may come away believing that new information has been arrived at with the aid of paranormal means.

In Frederick Nodder's case, it was methodical police work that brought him to justice. The involvement of Estelle Roberts, the 'psyhic detective', was a sideshow.

DRINK AND DRUG MURDERS

Drugs and drink are fuelling violent crime in Nottingham-shire. The Home Office has named the county as the fifth most violent place in England and Wales after Gwent, London, Greater Manchester and the West Midlands. During the financial year 1st April 2000 to 31st March 2001 eleven murders were committed in Nottinghamshire, according to official police figures.

It is estimated that drug-related crime costs Nottingham-shire at least £70 million a year. The most common offences associated with drugs are shoplifing, thefts from cars, burglary and prostitution. Some police officers will privately tell you that drugs could account for up to 80% of crime committed in the county. Recent research by the Arrestee Drug Abuse Monitoring (ADAM) project, which was partly carried out in Nottingham, found that 69% of people arrested during January 1999 tested positive for at least one drug – about 40% of them had taken heroin, cocaine, or crack cocaine.

There were 13,371 attacks on people in Nottinghamshire last year, the majority of which were drink-related. The city of Nottingham is believed to have a higher proportion of licensed premises per square mile than anywhere else in the country. The charity Alcohol Concern believes that twice as many people are addicted to alcohol in Britain as to illegal and prescription drugs. Up to five per cent of Britons can be

During the year 1st April 2000 to 31st March 2001, there were 11 murders in Nottinghamshire. A finger-tip search at a crime scene is expensive but can make the difference between securing a conviction or not.

classed as alcoholics, according to Alcohol Concern. Drugs and alcohol are behind much violent crime, and when intoxicants are a factor in a murder that crime is often more vicious, and cruel, as the following cases show.

In July 1998 Paul Hufton was given a life sentence for stabbing a woman and throwing her from a twelfth floor flat. The court was told that the dead woman – 36-year Susan Hooton – had been stabbed in the face and neck seven times.

In December 1997 Susan Hooton, her uncle Fred Hooton and Paul Hufton, 42, were enjoying a drinking session in Hufton's flat at Burrows Court, Sneinton. All three had consumed a lot of alcohol. At some point Hufton got involved in an argument with Miss Hooton in the kitchen. As drink fanned the flames of the row into a raging fury,

Hufton grabbed a 5-inch kitchen knife and in frenzy stabbed Susan in the face and neck. He then picked her up, pushed her over the sink and out through the window. Despite the appalling injuries to her face and neck medical evidence at the trial showed Susan was still alive when she was thrown from a window almost 200 ft from the ground.

Hufton was arrested soon after the incident. Faced with the awful reality of what had happened he accepted that he could have been responsible for Susan's death, but has maintained that he couldn't remember what had happened in the kitchen. Psychiatric reports into Hufton's mental state showed there was nothing wrong with him. When he appeared at Nottingham Crown Court Hufton admitted the murder. His defence lawyer Brian Escott-Cox, QC, told the court in mitigation that Hufton was the first client he had ever had who had pleaded guilty to murder. In his closing remarks the trial judge, Mr Justice Ognall, told Hufton: 'You killed Susan Hooton in circumstances of quite exceptional brutality – the only redeeming feature is that you have pleaded guilty.'

On the night of 7th July 1998 16-year-old Paul Taylor was shopping with his mother at the Spar supermarket, Central Avenue, Stapleford. That same day 59-year-old Leslie Marshall, of Central Avenue, Stapleford, and 40-year-old Stephen Twells had been on an extended drinking session in Beeston. Marshall had been seen brandishing a knife in a pub and acting in a threatening manner. Marshall and Twells decided to get a taxi to the Spar supermarket in Stapleford to buy more drink.

Paul and his mother were outside the supermarket when the two drunks approached them. Paul became involved in a scuffle with the two men when Stephen Twells became abusive to Paul's mother. Leslie Marshall pulled a knife and fatally stabbed Paul through the heart. As he collapsed to the pavement Paul was kicked by his two attackers at least six times.

Marshall initially told police he had the knife as part of his job as a cleaner in a factory and, at his trial, initially pleaded guilty to the killing. Twells pleaded not guilty and was cleared of the teenager's murder after the prosecution's case collapsed. Marshall then tried to change his plea to not guilty before being sentenced; he also asked to change his legal team, claiming he had been misdirected in his plea. The trial judge, Judge Christopher Pitchers, rejected this appeal, concluding that Marshall had entered his guilty plea freely and had been represented by experienced counsel.

Passing sentence on Marshall, Judge Pitchers told him, 'It's clear you intervened completely unnecessarily in what in any event was a comparatively minor incident. You did what you had threatened to do to others in the public house and an innocent life has been lost. It's absolutely clear Paul Taylor had caused no trouble that night. He had done nothing wrong. All he did was what any decent young man would do – stand up for his mother.'

On 12th June 1999 heroin addict Michael Lester murdered a defenceless pensioner, Florence White, in a frenzied attack. Money to feed the killer's addiction was the motive. Lester had stalked his victim, following her home after she had collected her pension. Once at the house, in Valley Road, Bilsthorpe, 28-year-old Lester forced his way in, attacked Mrs White in the hallway, stabbing her more than 20 times, then dragged her body from the hallway through to the kitchen. After ransacking the house he fled the scene. Some 30 minutes later Graham White, Florence White's son, arrived and found his mother dead in a scene from a nightmare.

Graham was deeply traumatized by what he saw. He told reporters, 'Not an hour goes by when I do not think about it. It was horrible when I found mum. I immediately called for an ambulance and a neighbour who is a nurse but there was nothing anyone could have done. When I first saw her body and the blood I thought for about 20 minutes it had been an accident. Then I realised what had really happened. It was horrific. I could not sleep for a week. I will never forget it. I do not think a relative who discovers something like this can. Of course I think "what if I had been there sooner?". Constantly, you get feelings of guilt and anguish.'

The murder has had a deep and lasting impact on the close-knit community of Bilsthorpe. Many people in the village knew both Mrs White and Michael Lester. Mrs White had lived in the village for more than 50 years, her late husband Fred having worked at Bilsthorpe colliery. Described by neighbours as a quiet and unassuming lady, she was well liked in her community and used to attend St Margaret's church in the village, as did members of Michael Lester's family. Lester was sentenced at Nottingham Crown Court to life imprisonment with a further five years for burglary.

In similar circumstances, in September 1998, the body of 86-year-old Rene Swanwick was discovered by her son at her home in Priory Road, West Bridgford. She had been stabbed 27 times and slashed across her hands and arms as she bravely fought for her life. When police took members of Rene's family around the house to determine what had been stolen they found that the attackers had taken just a kettle, a clock-radio and a toaster.

The murder sent shock waves through the quiet suburban streets of West Bridgford. Rene had been a hard-working volunteer for the charity Age Concern for many years. She also helped run the Tuesday Club, a social group for pensioners. A major investigation was begun involving 50 officers from the major crime, forensic science, and support units, computer operations and the uniformed branch. Detective Superintendent Colin Warburton, who led the murder hunt, said: 'Rene Swanwick was a kind, nice woman who could never deserve such brutal injuries. You cannot get used to crimes like this and especially against someone who did everything she could to help others. Someone out there knows who committed this dreadful act . . .'

Between noon and 11.30pm on 23rd September 1998 Tony Gamble, 28, had been drinking in the King George pub, Nottingham, where his odd behaviour had caught the attention of barmaid Ann Molloy. She told police that on the night Mrs Swanwick had been killed she had had a weird conversation with one of the customers that had stayed in her memory. This customer had told her how he had murdered a man but had got away with a charge of manslaughter. She had served him in the King George during the day of 23rd September but had become very wary of him. Ann Molloy identified that man as Tony Gamble.

When charged with Rene Swanwick's murder, Gamble, of Eugene Gardens, The Meadows, denied murder but admitted manslaughter on the grounds of diminished responsibility. He had admitted the pitiful theft of a kettle, a clock-radio and a toaster. At his trial at Nottingham Crown Court the court heard that Gamble had gone into Mrs Swanwick's home and attacked her in her bedroom. Appearing for the defence, consultant psychiatrist Dr Neil Holden said Gamble suffered from a combination sociopathic disorder and emotional instability. Dr Holden said: 'He shows a disregard for others, in many ways he treats them as if they were inanimate objects. He reacts to obstacles in his path by aggressive behaviour. At times he has complained of voices in his head shouting at him. He does not regard the feelings of others therefore has little remorse for an act of violence against another party. My opinion is that his responsibility is substantially on the basis that he readily flares up with minimal provocation into extremes of violence, in my opinion much more so than an average individual.'

The court heard that during the day of 23rd September Tony Gamble had drunk eight to ten pints of beer between noon and closing time, just prior to the killing. However, in the opinion of Dr Holden alcohol had played only a 'minimal' role in the murder. The jury was also told that Gamble took a daily cocktail of the anti-depressant Prozac and tranquilizers. Further to this, Detective Superintendent Colin Warburton told the court that Gamble had been released from gaol just over a month before Mrs Swanwick was killed. The jury rejected Gamble's defence of diminished responsibility and found him guilty of murder. He was sentenced to life imprisonment.

THE MYSTERY OF THE SILVER ARROW AND THE LOST TOURNEY FIELD OF BLYTH

A recent survey among American tourists revealed that Sherwood Forest was third in their list of places to see in England, behind London and York. The forest's association with Robin Hood makes it a 'place of legend'. Indeed, throughout the county of Nottinghamshire place names and story telling still link the legends of Robin Hood to real locations. Tourist leaflets and guide book offer the visitor a wealth of places with a Robin Hood connection. I think I can add one more: the place where Robin won the Silver Arrow.

The Legend of the Contest for the Silver Arrow has long fascinated me. The story tells of how the Sheriff of Nottingham holds an archery contest as a ruse to capture Robin Hood. The prize for the best archer is an arrow made of purest silver. On the day of the contest Robin fails to show up, much to the disappointment of the crowd and of the sly sheriff. However, a stranger in a ragged cloak and hood beats all comers, including the sheriff's best archers, and wins the prize. The sheriff is suspicious and as the humble stranger receives the arrow he is seized by soliders and exposed as Robin Hood in disguise. Robin, with the aid of his outlaw band, makes a dramatic escape, carrying off both Maid Marian and the Silver Arrow. I suggest that this contest didn't take place in Nottingham, as is often portrayed in books and films, but was held at Blyth in the north of the county.

Blyth was on the northern fringe of Sherwood in Robin's

Robin Hood is still a popular folk hero.

time. It lies on three significant routes: the Old Great North Road, the ancient road between London and York, 'Stone Street', the ancient track-way running to Nottingham, and the main route between Sherwood and Barnsdale, Robin's other famous forest haunt. Blyth appears as a place name in many Robin Hood stories, ancient and modern.

In 1088 the Norman knight Roger de Busli built an important Benedictine monastery at Blyth, which could possibly provide a link with two of Robin Hood's associates. The priory belonged to the priory of St Katherine in Rouen and was manned chiefly by Norman monks. Friar Tuck it seems would not have been out of place there. Dom. David Knolls, in *The Religious Orders in England*, describes how in 1287 a 'criminous monk' was sent back to Rouen, followed by another 'undesirable' the following year.

The first mention we have of Maid Marian comes from a 13th century French poem, which has her as a shepherdess and Robin as a shepherd. Is there a French connection here – a link between the monks on the edge of Sherwood and this poem? A tenuous one perhaps; however, returning monks, particularly those of the 'criminous' and 'undesirable' variety, might well have spread exciting stories about the exploits of an outlaw robber band operating in the forest near their old priory. They may have come into contact with the outlaws first hand.

Blyth was the site of a Royal Tourney field. Tourneys were spectacular events where the best and bravest showed off all manner of martial skills at contests staged for the entertainment of the royal court. Unlicensed tourneys did take place irregularly, but the venues for the most prestigious events were the Royal Tourney Fields.

Tourneys were great money-spinners for the crown. With a prize such as the silver arrow the opportunity for a fat profit would not have been missed. Fees for those attending such events are recorded as follows: for earls 20 marks, for barons 10 marks, for landed knights 4 marks, knights without land 2 marks; further, the Archbishop had to provide the two clerks and two knights to exact the oaths and fees from the contestants.

Blyth was one of only five places in the whole kingdom licensed by Richard I for the holding of public tournaments. It was licensed on 22nd August 1194 and is known to have

Robin, with the aid of his outlaw band, makes a dramatic escape, carrying off both Maid Marian and the Silver Arrow.

continued as a tournament field well into the 14th century: there is an existing licence granted by Edward III in 1328. This covers the right period for Robin Hood to have completed there.

The exact location of the tourney field has been lost. However, the Rev J Stacye, in his article, 'On the Site of the Blyth Tournament Field', suggests that the ground was between Blyth itself and the hamlet of Styrrup. Stacye points out that five roads converge here and one field in particular offers a natural amphitheatre of rising ground, known as the 'Stere banke'. This is further supported by the name of an adjoining field, 'the Gallant Steads', which was pasture and is recorded as 'enclosure for the war-horses of the knights.'

If Robin won the Silver Arrow, as legend has it, he would surely have done so at the Royal Tourney Field at Blyth. Like Sherwood Forest itself, legends of Robin Hood change and grow. They do not die, like leaves in autumn, but live on in the imaginations of each succeeding generation like the new shoots in spring, a little changed perhaps but part of the same continuum.

A MOST DANGEROUS MAN

In June 1993 Michael Beniston Sams was sentenced to life imprisonment for murder, kidnap and unlawful imprisonment; he was further sentenced to four ten-year terms on blackmail charges. Five different police forces were involved in the hunt for Sams, at the time Britain's most wanted criminal.

Sams has been described by the noted criminal psychologist Paul Britton as a psychopath. In essence this means that Sams is not mentally ill but has a behavioural disorder which manifests itself in acts of violence and sexual perversion. In July 1991 Sams murdered teenager Julie Dart. He threatened to murder many more innocent people by sabotaging a train, and he threatened to plant firebombs in shopping centres. When he kidnapped estate agent Stephanie Slater police feared she too would be murdered within 48 hours of her capture.

Michael Sams, from Sutton-on-Trent, ran a tool repair business from a workshop in Salmon's Yard, tucked away just off Newark's busy Castlegate. A proficient electrical engineer, Sams has an almost obsessive fascination for railways which he would use later to aid his getaways. Sams has been married three times. His first marriage was to Susan Oake, when she was just eighteen and he was twenty. They split up after 12 years of marriage when Sams became violent. In his younger days Sams had served a nine-month sentence for car theft. Whilst in prison he developed a cancer in his right leg, which had to be amputated below the knee. As a result Sams harboured a deep-seated resentment of the criminal justice system. Cunning and highly intelligent he took pleasure in planning crime. Kidnap, murder and extortion began as fantasies, games that Sams played in his mind against the police.

In July 1993 19-year-old Julie Dart was playing a dangerous game, dabbling in prostitution. Julie needed extra money to pay off a debt that was hindering her application to join the army. She had gone to Chapletown, the notorious red-light district in Leeds, and asked prostitutes how much to charge and where to take clients. Tragically, as Julie street-walked on Spencer Place, Chapletown, Michael Sams was cruising the city looking for a girl to kidnap. Some time after 11.30 pm on Tuesday 9th July Sams abducted Julie Dart and drove her to his workshop in Newark. He had prepared a makeshift prison for his victim from a wheelie-bin.

On Friday 12th July Julie's boyfriend, Dominic Murray, received a letter from Julie telling him to inform the police and her mother that she had been kidnapped. Police received a similar letter with the demand for £145,000 in used notes and for a further £5,000 to be deposited in two bank accounts to secure Julie's safe release. Further to this, if the kidnapper's demands were not met Julie would be killed and a firebomb planted in a city shopping centre to prove the kidnapper's determination. This would be followed by another kidnap and another ransom demand. The letter instructed police to send a female officer to New Street Station, Birmingham and wait in a call box on Platform 9. On Monday 15th July at precisely 7 pm she would be contacted and given further instructions. Following the instructions to the letter so as not to alarm the kidnapper a female officer waited for the call. The call came some six minutes late, but the line went dead immediately it was answered.

In July 1993, Leeds teenager, Julie Dart, was playing a dangerous game.

Three days later, on a disused railway cutting near Easton, Lincolnshire, a farmer found the body of a young woman wrapped in a pink and white sheet and tied up with green rope. The body was identified from dental records as Julie Dart's. Forensic examinations revealed some key facts. Julie had been killed by a series of blows to the back of the head followed by strangulation with a ligature. The body had been dumped at the scene only hours before its discovery. Although decomposition had begun there was little evidence of insect activity that would be expected given the time of year. Experts thus concluded that the body must have been kept in a sealed container of some kind before being taken to the railway cutting.

Sams began a bizarre letter campaign to police threatening to commit further violent crimes. He was plainly seeking to engage police in some kind of battle of wills and probably saw himself as some kind of criminal mastermind. The result was quite the reverse – a shambles of false starts. On

Monday, 22nd July, West Yorkshire Police received another letter from the kidnapper. He expressed his regret that, in his words, 'Julie had to be killed.' Sams had been monitoring the news media. As no reports of the discovery of Julie's body had been made he offered to tell the police the location of the body if they didn't find it within days. In the letter Sams gave details of how he had killed Julie, tying her up, beating her unconscious with multiple blows to the back of the head and strangling her. Seeking to set the agenda Sams promised to continue his campaign until he got the ransom money and promised to demonstrate his firebomb within two weeks. In the letter Sams told police, 'Words will never be able to express my regret that Julie Dart had to be killed, but I did warn what would happen if anything went wrong . . . I still require the same monies as before under the same conditions, if you want to avoid serious fire damage and a further prostitute's life.'

Following a second handwritten letter, police again attempted to comply with Sams' instruction. On Tuesday 30th July, at 8.30 pm, a female officer again waited at a phone box, this time at Leicester Forest East Services on the M1. When she answered the call the taped instructions played to her were inaudible. When the officer told the kidnapper this the line went dead.

Another letter arrived on Thursday 1st August arranging a repeat attempt on Tuesday 6th August. However, police received a type-written letter on 5th August explaining that the kidnapper hadn't been able to find a suitable hostage. (Police kept the rendezvous anyway but no call came.) This letter arranged for another call to be made to Leicester Forest East services on Wednesday the 14th. Having previously given the police the run around, this time the kidnapper was in earnest.

When the female officer answered the phone the kidnapper claimed to be holding hostage a prostitute called Sarah Davies. Sams was bluffing but the police could take no chances. From Leicester Forest East he directed police to a phone box in Wakefield.

When the next call came the officer had a problem with the receiver and the line went dead. Had this communication breakdown not occurred, the police would have been directed to a package that had been placed under a motorway bridge.

Unaware of the operation West Yorkshire Police were conducting, South Yorkshire Police had received notice of this suspicious looking package. The bomb squad, sent to investigate, blew it up. The package was then discovered to have been an envelope inside a tin attached to a white-painted brick. The envelope had contained more directions. A further envelope was found in a call box near Barnsley.

On 19th August West Yorkshire Police received a letter with a Grantham postmark from Sams explaining that he had abandoned his plans when police had closed the M1 during the bomb scare. Sams felt compelled to give the police more information about the murder of Julie Dart. He told police he had kept the body in a wheelie bin and, due to the hot weather, decomposition had been rapid. Immediately after he killed her Sams had wrapped Julie's head in a towel. When he took the towel off, her hair, stuck to the blood on the towel, had come away. Initially police had suspected the hair had been cut off as some kind of hideous trophy. Sams told police he transported the body in a wheelie bin to where it was dumped near Easton.

It was October 1991 before Sams wrote to police again. He couldn't resist the temptation to bait the police about their lack of progress in catching him. Menacingly, Sams suggested that, as the sentence for one murder was the same as for two, which is incorrect, he would again kidnap and kill a prostitute if £145,000 ransom wasn't paid. The same female officer was again instructed to wait at a call box, this time on platform 3 of Carlisle Railway Station, at 8 pm on 21st October. No call came. Sams then tried exhorting £200,000 from British Rail by threatening to derail a passenger train.

This having failed he planned another kidnap.

On Wednesday 22nd January Stephanie Slater, sales negotiator for Shipways Estate Agents, had an appointment to meet a Mr Bob Southall to show him round an empty property on Turnberry Road, Great Barr. Twenty-five-year-old Stephanie had not been in the office when Mr Southall made the appointment. When she arrived he was standing outside the house carrying a clipboard and appeared to be surveying the rather run-down house. The viewing continued as normal until they reached the bathroom. Sams distracted Stephanie and when her back was turned pulled a chisel and a knife from his coat. Sams forced Stephanie into the bath and pressed the knife to her throat. Stephanie realised that in this situation compliance was the safest option, so in an effort to calm her attacker she told him, 'All right, all right, calm down. You've got me. Remember I'm human. Please don't kill me.' It seemed to work. Sams then tied her wrists together and put sunglasses with very thick dark lenses over her eyes, and ordered her out of the bath. As she got up the glasses fell off and Sams, fearing future identification, yelled at her not to look at him. Stephanie looked away from his face and Sams put the glasses back on. He then tied a noose around her neck. Stephanie feared she going to be hanged in the empty house. Sams frog-marched her downstairs, blind-folded her with her own scarf, gagged her and loosely tied her legs so she could just about walk.

Sams had laid his plans well. At the back of the property was a garage. Sams had forced the door and parked his car inside before Stephanie had arrived. He had worked out that by leaving the house via the patio doors to the back garden he could get Stephanie into the garage and into his car with little risk of being seen. Once in the passenger seat Stephanie was tied with a rope under her chin, effectively doubling her up, stopping her from sitting upright. Sams covered her with a blanket and a coat and placed a heavy toolbox in her lap to prevent further movement and set off for Newark.

At some point on the journey Sams stopped the car, asked Stephanie her name, and told her to call him Bob. Sams then got Stephanie to make a tape demanding ransom from her employers. Sams told Stephanie exactly what to say. Her boss, Kevin Watts, was to pay the ransom and if all went according to plan Stephanie would be released on Friday 31st January. The tape was then posted.

Darkness had fallen by the time they arrived at Salmon's Yard, Newark. Sams guided the bound and gagged Stephanie into his workshop, handcuffed her at the wrists and ankles and tied her to a chair. Warning her to keep quiet, he went to get them some food, returning within 15 minutes with fish and chips. Terrified, Stephanie could barely eat. She was then untied and told to lie on a mattress on the floor. Sams then stripped her and raped her. Still gagged and blind-folded Stephanie was dressed in a pair of men's jeans and two woollen pullovers. She was then forced to wriggle into a wooden box inside the wheelie-bin. It was incredibly cramped and Stephanie had to contort herself to fit. She was then handcuffed to a bar positioned above her head and was told that if she pulled against this bar rocks would crash down and kill her. Sams also told her that the box was electrified and would shock her if she moved. Sams then shut the lid of the wheelie bin and locked it, leaving Stephanie to a tortuous night of cold, discomfort and blind terror.

The next day when Sams let her out Stephanie's arms had gone dead and he had to rub them before she could hold a drink. Throughout her ordeal Stephanie took care not to provoke her kidnapper, seeing compliance as her best hope of survival. She took every opportunity to remind Sams she was a real person with a family and a life. This seemed to work: Sams made her prison box more comfortable so she could at least lie flat. He told Stephanie that if everything went according to plan and he got the ransom money she would be released as planned on January 31st.

Stephanie suffered an eight-day ordeal, by day handcuffed

to a chain just long enough to allow her to reach a chair and a bucket, by night locked in the wheelie-bin. Sams left Radio 2 playing all day, but Stephanie could still make out what appeared to be the sounds of a shop bell and customers talking with Sams. Through conversations with Sams Stephanie sought to build some kind relationship with her captor in an attempt to make him less ready to kill her. Sams invented a violent accomplice who, he told Stephanie, would kill her if she disobeyed instructions and removed her blindfold. Sams was acting out a sick fantasy in which he was both protector and tormentor of Stephanie.

Kevin Watts, Stephanie's boss, received the taped ransom demand and contacted the police. They imposed a media blackout of all reporting of the kidnap. They were convinced that the man who had Stephanie Slater was the same man who had killed Julie Dart. Forensic evidence suggested that Sams had murdered Julie Dart within 48 hours of her capture. At this stage of the inquiry police had also made the link to the unsolved abduction of estate agent Suzy Lamplugh in 1986. Suzy had disappeared after meeting a Mr Kipper at an empty property.

The owners of Shipways Estate Agents, Royal Insurance, arranged to pay the £175,000 ransom for Stephanie. Sams had planned the drop for Wednesday January 29th and wanted Kevin Watts to act as courier of the ransom money. Over 1,000 officers were marshalled from forces across the midlands to take part in the operation to apprehend the kidnapper. Detectives privately feared that Stephanie was already dead. Kevin Watts, bravely rejecting an offer from the police to find him a stand-in, was fitted with a bullet-proof vest and a tracking device was secreted in the bag containing the money. At 3.25 pm, just as it was getting dark, Sams phoned the Shipways office, and told Kevin Watts to drive to Glossop. A two-way radio had been fitted in Kevin's car; each time Kevin got an instruction he was to repeat it aloud to officers listening in.

Sams used his in-depth knowledge of railways to plan the ransom drop; he wanted a roadway running over a disused railway line along which he could make his escape once the money had been dropped down from above. He found the ideal spot just off the M1, near Dodworth west of Barnsley, where Blacker Green Lane passes over the *Dove Valley Trail*. Sams had placed a wooden tray up on the old railway bridge with a rope attached, trailing down to the railway track below. Once the bag with the money in was on the tray Sams would only have to pull on the rope to bring it down to himself. To effect a quick getaway Sams had bought a Suzuki moped along in his car.

Kevin Watts was following instructions; from Glossop he was sent to Barnsley, from there to Sheffield and finally to a phone box in Dodworth. He was then directed down Blacker Green Lane. Fog and the winter darkness were making driving difficult, but then he came across a traffic cone in the road with a message attached telling him he had just 60 seconds to get to the bridge, find the tray and place the money on it. Some 60 feet below in the cover of the fog and gloom Sams waited for the sound of Kevin's car reversing away. He jerked the rope and the money fell at his feet. He made good his escape despite coming off the moped three times.

The police operation was a disaster: communications had broken down and officers had got lost in the fog; they had lost the money and they had lost the kidnapper. There seemed little hope of saving Stephanie now – the kidnapper had no reason to keep her alive and he risked her incriminating him as long as she still lived.

Locked in the wheelie-bin Stephanie could only hope the night had gone well for her captor and he would release her as he had promised. When Sams returned she asked him how everything had gone. Sams, seeking to maintain the subterfuge, told her that his partner had fallen off his moped three times but they had the money. Sams told Stephanie that he would be taking her to her parents in Birmingham and that she was to dress in her own clothes once more. For the whole time on the long journey to Birmingham Stephanie was in mortal fear that Sams would change his mind and kill her. Although he had allowed her to take off the blindfold she carefully avoided looking at him and kept her eyes closed much of time. Stopping just a few hundred yards from her parents' house, Sams insisted on a goodbye kiss, a sickening last humiliation for Stephanie but a sure sign of her success in building a relationship with her captor, a strategy that probably saved her life.

Just before 1 am on 30th January Stephanie's parents answered the frantic ringing of their doorbell to find their daughter home safe. At a press conference Stephanie admitted her 'sheer absolute terror', of not knowing what was going to happen to her. Smiling weakly for the TV and press cameras, the former pupil of Churchfields High School, West Bromwich, told how she lived on soup, porridge and Kit-Kats during her eight-day ordeal. 'I don't know how I kept going, I just tried not to think what was happening to me,' she said.

Stephanie told police all she could about her kidnapper, but she couldn't bring herself to report the rape. Only much later could she tell the full horror of her captivity in her book, *Beyond Fear: My Will to Survive*.

After the failed operation and the loss of £175,000 to the kidnapper, changes were made to the police task force working on the case. Assistant Chief Constable Tom Cook was put in charge of a joint operation between West Midlands and West Yorkshire police. Tom Cook wanted to entice the kidnapper into giving police more information and so told the media that he expected to hear from the kidnapper, who would not be able to resist boasting of his success over the police. He was absolutely right and Sams sent a three-page letter to the police and copies to the media and to Julie Dart's mother, Lynn Dart. In the letter Sams gloated over his success with the Stephanie Slater kidnap but

Michael Sams' house at Sutton-on-Trent, near Newark. Seen here during filming for a BBC documentary on the case.

denied being the railway extortionist or the killer of Julie Dart. However, he gave himself away by making the same spelling and typographical mistakes throughout all his letters to police. He had spelt ransom as 'ransome' – perhaps subconsciously alluding to Newark's biggest employer, the bearing makers, Ransome, Hoffman and Pollard. Other oblique references to Newark were included in his letters, giving hints as to his location, though these weren't picked up at the time. Another tale-tale error was on the envelope; Sams had written 'Millgate' rather than 'Millgarth' Police Station. Millgate is a street in Newark near to Sams' workshop. These constant errors in correspondence with police eventually identified Sams as the perpetrator of all three crimes.

Police circulated an artist's impression of the kidnapper drawn from Stephanie's description. Seeing this picture in a newspaper set the first seed of suspicion in the mind of Susan Oake; it reminded her of her ex-husband Michael Sams. Her suspicions grew as she read the article. The kidnapper was said to have worn a jacket with a railway motif, have a keen interest in railways, and knowledge of electronics. Then on 17th February she met Sams at his father's funeral, to which, she noticed, he drove a red Metro. A few days later Susan Oake read in a newspaper that a witness had seen a vermilion Metro near to the Slater family home on the night Stephanie was released. From the newspaper Susan noted that the BBC *Crimewatch* programme would be broadcasting a recording of the kidnapper's voice. Susan was out on the night the programme was shown but asked her son to record it for her on video. When she had seen the programme and heard the voice she no longer had any doubts. The kidnapper was Michael Sams. Susan Oake contacted the police. On the morning of 21st February 1992 police officers called at the workshop in Salmon's Yard and arrested Sams. Under questioning he soon confessed to the kidnapping of Stephanie Slater but strenuously denied killing Julie Dart.

The trial took place during June of 1993 at Nottingham Crown Court. Sams pleaded guilty to the kidnap of Stephanie Slater. He pleaded not guilty to the murder of Julie Dart, not guilty to blackmailing Leeds police for her release and not guilty to blackmailing British Rail with his threat to derail a passenger train. In the course of the trial a witness told of hearing screams from the area of Castlegate, Newark after midnight in July 1991. The witness then saw Sams stagger out of his workshop with his head in his hands complaining of a headache. It emerged that Julie Dart was claustrophobic and may have resisted being forced into the wheelie-bin prison. It was suggested that Julie's fear of being enclosed may have compelled her to fight back and this resistance could have triggered Sams to murder her. The jury of eight women and four men took just over three and a half hours to deliberate on the verdict. They returned a unanimous verdict of guilty on all counts. Sams was sentenced to four separate life sentences and a further forty years for blackmail. In the opinion of the trial judge, given in his closing remarks, Sams is an extremely dangerous and evil man.

In the first week of his life sentence Sams confessed to the murder of Julie Dart. Apparently he had never blindfolded Julie as he had always planned to kill her.

In December 1994 Michael Sams claimed that he had killed Suzy Lamplugh, who had disappeared on July 28 1986 and was officially declared dead in 1994. Her body has never been found. Lamplugh 25, vanished after leaving her office in Stevenage Road, Fulham, to show a client known as Mr Kipper around a house in Shorrolds Road, about a mile away. Kipper was the maiden name of Sams' mother. After making inquiries police have rejected Sams' confession as a sick attention-seeking hoax. In May 2000 police announced that they are to reopen the Lamplugh case. A key witness has come forward with new evidence, leading officers from Scotland Yard's serious crime group to consider for the first time that Ms Lamplugh's disappearance may have involved more than one man. It was initially thought that the estate agent had got into a black BMW driven by 'Mr Kipper' at around 1 pm, but the new information contradicts this theory. They will now focus on a 'core group' of suspects. As part of the review, samples taken from the dead woman's car – fibres, hair and human tissue – will be subjected to DNA testing not available at the time of the initial investigation. The police acknowledged that some of their suspects were serving prison sentences for violent crime. Suzy's mother, Mrs Lamplugh, 63, runs a charitable trust in her daughter's name to advise young women on personal safety.

In 1997 Sams had eight years added to his four life sentences after taking a probation officer, Julia Flack, hostage at Durham prison. Sams, defending himself, told Durham Crown Court, 'She asked me for my name and that threw me. When I go into

Michael Sams.

the workshops I never give my name, I just walk straight in. It is a bit arrogant you might presume, but this is the way I am. Being a Category A prisoner, all prison officers should be able to recognise me by sight. I told her, "Sit down, put your hands on the table and you won't be killed." I know I said that because I had been rehearsing it all day. I wanted to stop her getting to the panic button. She did not comply and started fiddling.' Sams, now in his sixties, is considered one of the country's most troublesome prisoners in the system.

In January 2000 the Prison Service agreed to pay Michael Sams £3,548 in an out-of-court settlement over property lost during a move between jails. Sams had sued the Prison Service over the loss of six of his paintings, personal items, including cassette tapes, and loss of earnings incurred while he was being held in a prison segregation unit. Sams also claimed to have been 'unfairly' held in solitary confinement. The six paintings, mostly railway scenes, were valued at £500 apiece by a judge at an earlier hearing. The hearing was scheduled for 18th February 2000 and plans were drawn up for a special court hearing inside Whitemoor Prison, Cambridgeshire, to consider the case. Sams was again going to represent himself. However, the Prison Service decided it would be cheaper to settle the matter out of court than proceed with what might have been a lengthy court case. Sams accepted the offer but did not receive the money himself. The pay out was made to nominated recipients.

Sams' legal action follows legal challenges by other inmates at Woodhill over the gaol's top-security supervision unit built to house the most troublesome prisoners in the prison system. Inmates challenged the process for sending prisoners to the unit, where prisoners on the most basic level are kept in solitary confinement in cells furnished with cardboard furniture and concrete beds. Norman Brennan, Director of the Victims of Crime Trust, said that new laws were needed to stop inmates pursuing claims against the Prison Service.

Still fighting a personal war against authority, Sams is at present held in Durham prison and is still considered one of the country's most dangerous criminals.

THE STRANGE DEATH OF
HELEN DUNCAN

On the night of Monday, 29th October 1956 police
raided a séance in an upstairs room in West Bridgford,
Nottingham. The famous medium, Helen Duncan, was in
her trance state when the police burst in. As every medium
will tell you it is highly dangerous, even potentially fatal, to
suddenly break a medium's trance. Some 39 days later Helen
Duncan was dead.

In the early hours of the morning of Tuesday, October 30,
1956 Helen's husband, Henry Duncan, awoke in their home
in Edinburgh to find his wife standing by the bed, fully-
dressed. Henry knew something was seriously wrong. His
wife was deathly pale and obviously under some emotional
strain. Helen should have been in Nottingham that night;
Henry hadn't expected her back in Edinburgh so soon. He
asked what was the matter. With tears in her eyes Helen told
him she was leaving him after 40 years of marriage, but
could barely bring herself to do it. Henry was shocked and
reached for her hand. Helen vanished.

With a sense of foreboding Henry waited for the bad news
he was sure would come. Sure enough, just after 9 am a tele-
gram arrived from Helen's companion on the Nottingham
trip, Gert Hamilton, saying that the police had raided the
séance and Helen was seriously ill. They were coming back
to Edinburgh that day.

When Helen Duncan arrived home she was in considerable pain and suffering from shock. On her right breast was a burn approximately 18 cm across, and on her stomach a second burn about 12 cm across. A doctor was called and concluded that the injuries Helen suffered looked like electrical burns. The burns and her diabetic condition warranted admission to Edinburgh's Western General Hospital. Though she was released from hospital shortly afterwards her health deteriorated during November and she died on 6th December 1956. The death certificate gave the cause of death as diabetes and cardiac failure. The headline in the *Daily Express* of December 8th read, 'Medium's death blamed on raid'. Charles Loseby, the barrister who had defended Duncan in the famous 1944 'witchcraft' trial, told reporters, 'Helen Duncan was murdered!'

Did Helen Duncan really die because police broke her trance? Why was the séance raided at all? What really happened in West Bridgford that night?

Helen Duncan was born in Callendar, Scotland on November 25th 1897. Her husband, Henry, had been injured during the first world war and the Duncans had six children to feed. To sustain this large family and a disabled husband Helen worked in the local bleach factory by day and as a medium by night. Her speciality was physical mediumship, summoning actual physical phenomena whilst in trance state. In the 1930s and 1940s she was travelling the length of Britain holding regular séances in hundreds of Spiritualist churches and homes. During the years of the second world war, Helen lived in Portsmouth, the home of the Royal Navy. As the toll of war dead mounted Duncan became popular with the grieving relatives of lost sailors and merchant seamen. At a Duncan séance in 1943 the spirit of a dead sailor materialised for his mother; on his cap-band was the name 'HMS Barham'. The woman later telephoned the Admiralty to ask for confirmation that HMS Barham had sunk. Two naval intelligence officers subsequenctly visited the bereaved mother demanding to know the source of her information. She told them about Helen Duncan.

Official interest in Helen Duncan centred on allegations of fraud and on the potential hazard to security that her activities had become. By December 1943 she was being investigated by Detective Inspector Frederick Ford of the Portsmouth police. This no-nonsense detective of 16 years' service had received several complaints about Duncan and mounted a police surveillance operation on her. Significantly DI Ford consulted members of the Magic Circle to try to gain an understanding of how mediums operate. He found out that mediums and their assistants go to extraordinary lengths to gather information about their clients so as to provide revelations at sittings as if by supernatural means. This kind of intelligence gathering often involves listening in to conversations in pubs, shops and queues, talking to neighbours and friends – anything to gather information to use in a séance. Duncan had contacts in the dockyards and she knew many relatives of serving seamen. This is how she had picked up her information about HMS Barham. However, in war time, when 'Careless Talk Cost Lives', such intelligence gathering was highly dangerous. Indeed, Duncan had been warned by Charles Burrell, a dockyard worker and medium, that she was on thin ice. Burrell had threatened to report her to the police unless she stopped her séances. However, Duncan continued advertising in the *Portsmouth Evening News*.

On 19th November 1944, police raided one of Helen's séances. The subsequence trial began on Thursday, 23rd March 1944 in Court No. 4 of the Blitz-damaged Old Bailey and remains one of the most famous in British legal history. At the trial Arthur West, the Chief Constable of Portsmouth, summed up the whole issue of Duncan's transgressions: 'This is a case where not only has she attempted and succeeded in deluding confirmed believers in spiritualism, but she has tricked, defrauded and preyed upon the minds of a certain credulous section of the public who have gone to these meetings in search of comfort of mind in their sorrow and grief, many of whom left with the firm conviction that the memory of the dead had been besmirched. She thought fit to come to Portsmouth, the first naval port of the world, where she would find many bereaved families, and there she practised her trickery.' West made explicit reference to Helen Duncan 'having transgressed the security laws, in a naval connection, when she foretold the loss of one of His Majesty's ships long before the fact was made public'. Helen Duncan was found guilty under the terms of the Witchcraft Act 1735; she was the last person to be tried under that law in Britain. She was sentenced to nine months in London's Holloway Prison.

In October 1956 Helen Duncan had been invited to stay with a Mr Timmins, a chiropodist and healer in West Bridgford, to conduct a séance. In an upstairs room Mr Timmins arranged his sitters as Helen took her place, and the ordinary white light was switched to red. After the company had sung the hymn 'The Lord is My Shepherd' Helen Duncan went into her trance and her spirit guide, Albert, greeted the sitters. Over the next twenty minutes two spirits allegedly made contact – a deceased local doctor and an Austrian pianist. Then came the knock at the door and police officers with cameras burst into the room. Helen Duncan, who had been still in a state of trance, appeared to faint and fall to the floor, her face ghastly pale. But in the voice of Albert she reassured her companion, Gert, that she was not dead. Still in a state of collapse Duncan was lifted onto a bed by several officers. She was then cautioned.

The police searched the room for 'props' – beards, masks, shrouds. They searched Gert and Helen's suitcases but found nothing significant. Helen Duncan was questioned for over an hour and statements were taken from everyone in the house. Helen and Gert were genuinely frightened by the prospect of prison. Helen could expect a much longer sentence for a second offence and her health wasn't good.

Making little progress with their search the police released Duncan without charge.

On 10th November, *Psychic News*, in an open letter to the Chief Constable of Nottingham, accused his officers of behaving like the Gestapo and quoted the Fraudulent Mediums Act of 1951, namely that mediumship is only an offence if intent to deceive could be proved. At the West Bridgford raid police hadn't been able to prove fraud. To help their investigations officers examined the files of the 1944 Duncan trial to see whether new information could be gleaned. Nottinghamshire police felt they had a case under the Fraudulent Mediums Act, though prosecutions using this law were very rare and remain so to this day. The Chief Constable of Nottingham wrote to Duncan in mid November informing her that they had passed their files on to the Director of Public Prosecutions.

In the meantime Helen Duncan's health was failing. Her doctor was prescribing increasing doses of morphine to allay the pain from angina and the two electrical burns. She died on 6th December before the DPP could proceed with the case.

As the records of this case are still not in the public realm the reasons for the police raid remain obscure. Were police tipped off about the séance? What is certain is that they were unable to find any immediate evidence of fraud. Helen Duncan was certainly badly affected by the raid. Was this really the result of the violent re-absorption of ectoplasm? Her doctor's view was that her injuries were electrical burns. It seems probable that some concealed device was used to fake her 'physical mediumship'. Could such a device concealed on her person have over-heated or malfunctioned during the police raid, causing the burns? Could the burns have been acid burns from batteries perhaps? Although the police questioned Helen Duncan thoroughly she was never strip-searched. Being very afraid of another prison sentence she would have been desperate to conceal a fraud, so might have suffered the burning from some hidden device all through her questioning. Certainly the pain and distress of those burns would have put her failing health under considerable strain.

In the words of the Witchcraft Act of 1735, the offence of being a medium was of 'pretending to exercise or use a kind of conjuration' and of 'pretending to be a Medium'. A bronze bust of Duncan, on display in her hometown of Callander, still causes controversy. Helen Duncan remains a figure of fascination and attempts are still being made to secure a posthumous pardon for her.

ACKNOWLEDGEMENTS

I thank the excellent staff of Nottinghamshire's libraries and archives for their outstanding assistance. My grateful thanks also go to archaeologists Ms Jenny Challis and Ms Nicola Jennings for their expert advice and for their patient proof reading; to parapsychologist Kieran O'Keefe of the University of Hertfordshire for his specialist advice regarding psychic detectives; and to the many contributors, artists, historians and journalists without whose help and assistance this project would not have been possible.